WHY THE
GRATEFUL DEAD
MATTER

WHY THE GRATEFUL DEAD MATTER

Michael Benson

• • •

ForeEdge

ForeEdge

An imprint of University Press of New England

www.upne.com

Manufactured in the United States of America

Designed by Eric M. Brooks

Typeset in Calluna by Passumpsic Publishing

For permission to reproduce any of the material in this book,
contact Permissions, University Press of New England, One Court Street,
Suite 250, Lebanon NH 03766; or visit www.upne.com

Library of Congress Cataloging-in-Publication Data

Benson, Michael.

Why the Grateful Dead matter / Michael Benson.

pages cm

ISBN 978-1-61168-851-1 (pbk.)

ISBN 978-1-61168-924-2 (ebk.)

1. Grateful Dead (Musical group) 2. Rock music—
United States—History and criticism. I. Title.

ML421.G72B46 2015

782.42166092'2—dc23   2015030862

5 4 3 2 1

To
Jerry, Pig,
Keith, Brent,
and Vince . . .
now they *know*

Contents

Illustrations follow page 80

WHY THE
GRATEFUL DEAD
MATTER

Introduction
LIGHT THE SONG

Light the song with sense and color, hold away despair.
Robert Hunter, "Terrapin Station"

Light the song, and pass it around. Don't bogart. Let it shine, let it shine, stoke it on a Palo Alto stage, until that fire reaches the mountain in Concord, the magnolia fields down by the river, becomes a conflagration of the heart stretched from south Colorado to the west Texas town of El Paso, the twilit purple plain of Wichita, all the way to Europe and the Pyramids of Egypt under a lunar eclipse. Stoke it until it envelops the earth with an accelerando of peace.

And *that's* the Grateful Dead, not just a band that played songs, sold records, and gave concerts, but a band of sorcerers, conjurers of a rare and different tune, music with a heartbeat and breath, with the perfect tension between dissonance and resonance, suspension and completion, a cynosure for the huddled masses, tie-dyed angel music for spinning the sacred dance of life as a falling leaf at the jubilee, a rolling away of the dew, a movement and groove that gets into the fiber of your skull, spreads like ripples on still water, grows roses along a trellis of bones, messes with the gears of your body clock until you're on a long, strange pilgrimage jonesing to find the forty-five-minute "Sugaree," waving that flag, driving that train, holding away the despair with a cloak of space and drums, lightening the load until you get up and fly away.

You don't have to take my word for it. The famous mythologist Joseph Campbell (his book *The Power of Myth* is required reading in many college courses) went to a Dead show and said the music was the antidote to the Damoclean sword of nuclear war.

Why do the Dead still matter? Why will they *always* matter? Sure, because of the genius music, years of trippy listening pleasure—Jerry Garcia's beam-me-up-Scotty leads and achingly sad vocals, Phil Lesh's intricate bass lines weaving in and out of everything including the sound system, Bobby Weir's strong masculine vocals and truly weird and wonderful second-chair guitar, the growling blues of Pigpen, the musicality and lightness of Keith and Donna Godchaux, and the *Apocalypse Now* rhythm section, the devils, Bill Kreutzmann and Mickey Hart, all of whom we'll be on a first-name basis with from now on—but there's a rebel bad-boy social component as well. Their first fans thought they were bikers. The band matters because through it *the counterculture lived on*—ironic because the musicians were more piratical than political. They never turned a show into an antiwar demonstration. Although they were against all violence, their vision of show biz didn't involve causes. They just didn't like to follow rules and were constantly trying to get away with shit. But it didn't matter. The counterculture burbled urgently from deep fissures in the earth beneath the San Andreas Fault, and the Dead were swept away in the movement despite their apathy. They were too close to the crevasse to avoid the deep rift in society.

America came out of World War II a militaristic animal, intoxicated by its own might, its ability to push enemies around, to purge the world of evil. But the following generation, the kids coming of age in the 1960s, saw military solutions in a different light. The war in Vietnam had no real purpose; it had sprung up like a malignant weed through the cracks in Elm Street—Dealey Plaza, Dallas—where a crossfire disguised as a magic bullet burned Camelot to the ground. While America was spoon-fed Oswald pabulum, an undigested buzz of coup cabal grew into an electronic feedback wail—Dylan at Newport—and radicalized the American folkie-bohemian. Anti-Nam protests evolved smoothly from the preexisting Cold War academic beatnik movement to "ban the bomb." Like the war before it in Korea, Vietnam was a civil war, a north fighting a south, and there seemed no cause for the United States to intervene. What was it all about, anyway? Profit? *They* said it was about the "domino theory": if North Vietnam—and it's Red Chinese backers—were allowed to conquer South Vietnam, the other small countries of Southeast Asia would fall as well. To many, the theory seemed weak—who cared who owned the jungle? Eisenhower had warned of the military-industrial complex, which would one day come slouching toward Bethlehem. War without reason was a symptom of the behemoth. The younger generation believed that war existed only to make a few men rich, while sacrificing the lives of American boys who didn't have the connections to avoid the draft. American involvement in Vietnam was light until the so-called Gulf of Tonkin incident, in which it was reported that a North Vietnamese ship fired across the bow of an American ship, an act of aggression used by LBJ, sworn in on Air Force One on a terrible day in Dallas, as an excuse to escalate hostilities to the jangly tune of billions of dollars and more than 50,000 American lives. Finally, CBS newsman Walter Cronkite, "the most trusted man in America," said on the six o'clock news that the war was unwinnable. In order to show their dissatisfaction with the world the adults were creating, the youth of America grew their hair long, a fashion that began as Beatlesque but eventually became antimilitary. Youths began to take mind-altering drugs, which they were told by Timothy Leary, Aldous

Huxley, Ken Kesey, and so many others, would expand their consciousness. Like Jack Kerouac and the beatniks before them, they worshipped the road, all the roads that led to the next Dead show, psychic roads that led to enlightenment.

It was the birth of a movement, initially a fad of psychedelia,* from which the Dead were the last survivors.

*The Dead's contribution to hippie fashion is immeasurable. One quick example: Without the Grateful Dead there would be no tie-dye. It was about 1969 and Bobby was driving to his ranch when he picked up a hitchhiker looking for a place to crash. Weir said he could stay at the ranch if he stacked firewood. The guy turned out to be a good worker and bunked there for a while. He was also an artist who invented the tie-dying technique in which dye and cloth simulated the psychedelic patterns of colored-water-on-a-vibrating-membrane light shows. The Dead dug his stuff and began draping tie-dyed sheets over their amps and speakers during shows. And that was how it began. Millions of T-shirts and summer-camp experiments later, tie-dying is here to stay.

THEY'RE AN AMERICAN BAND

The Grateful Dead were made up of misfits, many of whom hung out in the same Northern California music store. They formed a band for the usual reasons, to attract women, for something to do, but unlike most garage bands—satisfied with three chords and high-school dances—they developed a seriousness of purpose that combined drug intake, a nerdy interest in sound technology, eclectic musical influences, a willingness to improvise, and talent, and turned it all into something resembling real ambition. Thus, they became charter members of the counterculture movement's noisiest wing—acid rock. They were joined by bands that, like the Dead, were weirdly named to convey their disregard for straight convention: Jefferson Airplane, Moby Grape, Quicksilver Messenger Service.

A lot of acid rock was electric folk, like the Byrds, but at a whole new freak-out level. The Dead heaped blues atop the mix, and later country, bluegrass, Americana. It was a time of strobe lights and many guitar solos. As the sixties progressed tumultuously, the movement became rich with all kinds of bands, many of whom played Monterey and Woodstock, then one by one dropped by the wayside while the Dead forged on, so many roads, pied with tie-dye and humming with love vibes.

They were American gypsies, and yet somehow the act didn't cross borders well. Perhaps customs was an issue. The Grateful

Dead never built a solid fan base outside of the United States. Even in Canada, there was a disconnect.

As Bobby Weir told Benjy Eisen of *Rolling Stone* in 2014, "We played in Mexico, but there weren't any Mexicans there."

The Dead played some of their best music in Europe in 1972, but the audiences sat there and stared, not totally comprehending, their hands folded in their laps even when Bobby begged them to get up and dance. How odd it was to hear the silence when Jerry dropped the F-bomb in "Wharf Rat."

No, the Dead are an American band, for American audiences the F-bomb kills every single time. They are just one of many advantages we Americans have over the rest of the world, and being a Deadhead is an act of patriotism. To find the reasons why, let's take a look at the symbols used in the band's most red, white, and blue song: "U.S. Blues."*

Words by longtime lyricist Robert Hunter, sung by Jerry, "U.S. Blues" is a rocker party song consisting largely of a list of people, places, symbols, objects, and situations to which the Dead are wedded in myth and legend. These things are, first, red, white, and blue—Old Glory herself. During a time when it was fashionable to burn the flag in protest of U.S. foreign policy, the Dead preferred to cling to the traditional symbol, but with the caveat that to recognize national flaws and to seek to fix them (or just get off the ride and do your own thing) is, in itself, a new and enlightened form of patriotism. Second, "Blue Suede Shoes," the rockabilly of Carl Perkins, and a song made famous by Elvis Presley. The song

---

*Before we start tugging apart art where there aren't any seams, let us register the disapproval of Dead lyricist Robert Hunter, who believes that it does disservice to a lyric to dismantle symbolism, symbols more intense without a verbal explanation, layered with multiple shades of subjectivity. It's like explaining a joke until it isn't funny anymore. And I won't do a lot of it, promise, but this one is for America.

can be seen as a musical bridge linking Big Joe Turner's shouted Kansas City blues, with the birth of rock 'n' roll, and it's assimilation into white culture. Third, Uncle Sam, a recruiting symbol for the military, now appropriated by a rock 'n' roll band to build a new army of shaggy revelers. (As we learn during the animated portion of *The Grateful Dead Movie*, the new Sam is a skeleton, but he still wears the same ol' hat.) Fourth, P. T. Barnum, a symbol of American show business, partly vulgar, partly a con job, always on the road, moving to a new city with the self-proclaimed Greatest Show on Earth. Fifth, Charlie Chan, a symbol of immigration, a wise old Chinese detective of the movies (although always played by a white man in heavy, racially offensive makeup), who traveled with his son, always played by an actual Asian, who spoke English with an American accent and called his father "Pop." The notion that immigrants are being celebrated here is supported by the line "Shake the hand that shook the hand," originally an Irish-American lyric in which the singer is bragging about the degrees of separation between himself and the first heavyweight boxing champion, the great John L. Sullivan. The chorus urges us to wave our flag wide and high, as patriotic as anything ever written by Irving Berlin or George M. Cohan. The song is happy, even joyous, which makes its title the sole touch of irony. What are the U.S. blues? Is there an undercurrent of sadness in the song? No, the closest it comes is poignant with a profound nod to the power hunger and immorality that really successful Americans (including even themselves perhaps) exhibit ("Run your life / steal your wife"). Maybe there's a touch of melancholy in the notion that summer is almost over, and the kids have to get back to school. But there would be other summers, and sometimes great things happened in the fall, so what the heck. According to Dennis McNally, the title is rather none of the above, but an inside joke, a jab by Hunter at Bobby. Weir and Hunter fought over the song

"One More Saturday Night," McNally says, because Bobby rewrote Hunter's lyrics and wanted to change the title of the song to "U.S. Blues." Hunter forbade it, removed his name from the songwriting credit, and wrote a new song for Jerry to sing. As it says in the song, "You can call *this* song the United States Blues."

OF JERRY GARCIA, SAVIOR

Professional storyteller Nick Newlin wouldn't be the man he is today without the Dead and, with his permission, we repeat his tale here. When Nick was seventeen he began to collect bootleg Grateful Dead cassette tapes. He was a Harvard freshman at the time, studying psychology—but it soon became clear that psych was not his thing. When he listened to the Dead he realized that they'd found their thing, and had made it magical. He wanted to find *his* thing, so he could make *it* magical, too. As destiny would have it, that fall, Nick's roommate taught him how to juggle, and juggling became his thing. From then on, when he wasn't doing schoolwork or going to class, he was practicing his juggling while listening to the Grateful Dead. Four years later, when his class graduated and his classmates began their suit-and-tie lives, Nick went on the road wearing a jester's hat and juggling at Renaissance fairs. As often as he could, he attended Dead concerts, sometimes accompanied by his middle-school friend André. He and André used to play a game: blindfolded, they would pop a tape in the tape player and guess which year the concert was from. (And to this day André and Nick still play that game while listening to the Grateful Dead channel on Sirius Radio, which beams commercial-free Dead music 24/7 from *space*.) He still has friends he made at Dead shows, and though the friendship was great, his favorite thing was always the music. The band was wildly eclectic, and always included in each show "Space," formless improvisation of one-group mind. There were times when it didn't work and the sound would devolve into nothingness. And when that happened, the band would "bear down like mules in the rain and work until they unearthed lotus blossoms of perfection," and those were the moments Nick lived for. There was always a point at each show when Jerry would sing a ballad so beautifully sad that the entire stadium would fall silent. By the time Nick turned thirty he had been to about seventy concerts and owned two hundred cassettes. One day he was outside Dallas at an event called Scarborough Fair where five times a day he juggled axes and flaming torches, when he had an accident, fell, severed his Achilles tendon, and incurred a shoulder injury that did not get better. Still, he stubbornly juggled on. The pain became worse and his orthopedist said, "I have no surgery for this. You are either going to have to stop juggling or your shoulder will not get better." Juggling was his one ticket to freedom. Without it he'd have to get a real job, probably wear a jacket and tie. He felt his inner light dimming. He called a friend, who advised him, "You know the drill, Nicky. Spin some tapes." He chose 12/31/78, the closing of Winterland. He particularly tuned in to Jerry Garcia's solo on "Wharf Rat" as the notes painstakingly climbed up the register, hit a peak and then fell back down again. Stubbornly, the notes once more began to climb. A second time they reached that same peak and fell. The third time, with an almost unbearable ferocity, he climbed again and Nick felt as if he were standing at the edge of a cliff ready to fall, and then Jerry played one clear note higher than the others. Bobby promptly echoed that tone, and Phil echoed it an octave below them. The Grateful Dead had saved Jerry (and Nick) by making a miraculous musical pyramid. Nick let go and the music carried him. As it turned out, he did have to stop juggling and he did return to grad school. But he studied theater and began directing plays with DC-area high-school kids. Today he is still in show business putting on shows for children featuring music, poetry, storytelling, and yes juggling, lots of juggling. Only now when he drops something and it goes skittering away, he picks up something else and tosses it up in the air. These days he doesn't need his cassettes anymore, he can stream any Dead concert at any time on his phone. There's an app for that. Today, according to the *New York Times*, there are nearly 2,200 Dead shows recorded and archived, out of perhaps 2,350 that they played. Considering the quantity of product, the Dead business people are doling out the *Dick's Picks* and the *Road Trips* at a leisurely pace, so that the demand for new product remains strong. The only cassette he kept was 12/31/78, because he never knows when he might need a helping hand.

DEAD SHOWS ARE LIKE
SNOWFLAKES

The difference between man and nature can best be explained by how we make copies. Man puts a document in a photocopier—or a car on an assembly line—and produces identical copies. Nature makes snowflakes, each unique.

And that's what makes Dead shows so *natural*—there are no two alike. The band couldn't play the same show twice if they tried. They are constitutionally and musically unable to even play a song the same way twice. Jerry thought it had to do with the band's "pathological antiauthoritarianism."

The concept of "jamming" was once limited to the realm of small smoke-filled jazz clubs. Popular music listeners considered improvisation a subset of the lunatic fringe. In 1966, if you went to see a rock 'n' roll show—be it by the Beatles, Stones, or Little Richard for that matter—you could rest assured that the show you saw was identical to the show those performers gave the night before and the one they'd give the next night. And the songs you heard would be reproduced as closely to the recorded versions as possible. Making it sound "just like the record" was the *goal*.

Just as every Dead show was unique, their rehearsals were different from those of other groups as well: the band didn't want to work out material—old or new—in too much detail. In other words, they should never learn to play a song by rote, or else it would become easy and that would be how the musicians played it from then on. What the Dead did was so much more complicated than that. Their rehearsals were fragmented, out of order to an outsider, as mere slivers of songs would be gone over, a suggestion made to keep the changes the same at one particular point to create a crowd-pleasing moment, another suggestion that the end of the second chorus be their launching point to explore the heights. The Dead never wanted to make a live performance sound like the record. They didn't even want their record to sound like a record, and early in their career had on occasion attempted to make a recording sound like a live performance, but with limited success.

Jerry was sometimes envious of other lead guitarists—for example, say, Joe Walsh of the Eagles, a really talented guy. Joe knew how to play all of the Eagles hits in one crowd-pleasing way, and this is what he did night after night. He could probably go over the shopping list in his pocket as he played, for all of the concentration a performance like that would require.

Jerry couldn't do that, it wouldn't be artistically charged the way a Dead show is, because what the Dead do is hard; maintaining the vertical space night after night is exhausting to the band, who must always be both performers and creators on stage, as individuals and as a unit. "When it's hard," Jerry complained to David Gans, "it's the hardest thing there is, but when it's easy it's magic."

They come to the show with a skeletal arrangement. They all agree on where the bones are. Then, each night, they playfully apply the flesh until they have a full-bodied song.

World-caliber chess players are gauged by the number of moves they can plan ahead, and for an improvising musician the rating system involves the number of bars, that is, musical measures, he or she can think ahead. Jerry said that when he was in the groove he knew exactly how long sixteen bars was going to be and how many notes be could play before he got there.

Bands that want to play "tight" and always hit their cues with precision, always know where the bars fall, the "one" followed by however many beats there are in that song's measure. Regarding that standard, the Dead have another rule, one which is shared by no other band, and that is: "The one is where you want it to be," and so this band that performs songs in shifting keys and time signatures, have agreed not to agree on where each measure starts and stops. You could call it "Zen and the Art of Grateful Dead Maintenance." Because of the complex rhythm system it is conceivable that not everyone is playing the same measure anyway, so who cares where the one falls? The odd time signatures are Mickey's fault. Mickey dug the tabla player Alla Rakha (who was best known as Ravi Shankar's percussionist), dug the combination of freedom and discipline, and the Eastern influence in the Dead's music was there to stay. When cones of telepathy lowered over their heads during a Dead show, the most frequent clairvoyance occurred at the back, with Billy and Mickey, who could (they have claimed) be in absolute mind-meld synch for up to sixty, seventy bars at a time.

Sure, it's hard, but they chose to do it because it's hard: to maintain in the format of the performance the elusive truth that is artistic freedom. The free-form ethic seeps through each song and into the sequence of songs, which also is in a state of flux while the show is going on. While the Allman Brothers Band, the Who, the Clash might have a set list taped to the floor of the stage, the Dead may change one song into another and then back again on the spot without more than a smidgen of foreknowledge or foreshadowing. They realize that just as the songs themselves with their lyrics and major and minor chords have an effect on the audience, so does the song order, with its changing progression of emotional tones.

At some point the lack of a predetermined set list became an issue with the sound and lights people. "At least tell us the first song so we can give the show a dramatic beginning," they begged. So, for a time, Bobby would give them the name of a song. Trouble was, nine times out of ten that wasn't the song they opened with.

They took the free-form nature of music from jazz clubs, where it lived just under low ceilings in curlicues of midnight-blue smoke, transposed it onto their own songs, and put it in football stadiums. They were the first jam band. Today, jam band is a *genre* on satellite radio. Let it snow.

THE DEAD ARE EPICUREAN

Dead biographer and longtime music historian Dennis McNally was writing for the Sunday magazine that accompanied the *San Francisco Chronicle*, called *California Living*, in September of 1980, when he noted the three main points of the Deadhead worldview:

- the warm sharing of a family;
- the hippie contempt for commerciality that makes them stubbornly condescending to most other rock bands; and
- a noisy but peaceful determination to have a good time.

During the Dead's early years the musicians used LSD to achieve a common wavelength, a oneness with the music, until they were no longer playing their instruments, the instruments were playing them. They were constantly seeking to create an "aural holograph," to use Jerry's metaphor.

Maybe it was a metaphor, maybe not. There have been other raps in which Jerry says he wants to use visible sound waves and electron spin resonance to create an *actual holograph*. A little bit of Owsley has worn off on Jerry—seeing sound, manifesting thoughts. Biographer David Gans referred to the aural holograph phenomenon as "a band with a mind of its own." Phil used plumbing to illustrate the concept, saying their group mind was merely a way of opening the valves so that music could flow through. Well, Scott Beauchamp, in an online article, argues that one-group mind was a product of a kind of bliss experienced both by the musicians *and* the audience. He writes in his article "Sometimes We Live No Particular Way But Our Own: The Grateful Dead and Epicureanism," that one-group mind hinges on a state of being the Epicureans called *ataraxia*, a state of tranquility that Bob Weir, again according to Beauchamp, achieves three and a half minutes into the version of "China Cat Sunflower/I Know You Rider" as performed in 1971 at Bucknell University. According to the Greek philosophers, ataraxia is achieved by:

- losing both faith in the afterlife and fear of death,
- avoiding malcontents, the angry, and those corrupted by power and opinion making (i.e., politicians),
- surrounding oneself with trustworthy and affectionate friends; and, most importantly,
- being virtuous, loving, and as good as your word.

Dead lyricist John Barlow once told David G. Dodd that ataraxia comes at the moment when the band stops playing the music and the music starts playing the band. Not only is ataraxia the key to the Dead being the Dead, but it is the key to the band's addictive nature for the totally ataraxic Deadheads. The moment for Bobby isn't so much visible on his face as by the sound of what he plays during "China/Rider." Weir in essence stops being the rhythm guitarist, but rather adds "texture" to Jerry's lead while "pushing his own melodic ideas to the surface." This evolves into a second lead guitar that Beauchamp says is "more traditional than Jerry's, [but] definitely searing, seductive, and enigmatic." Beauchamp realizes that the historical record is not teeming with odes to Bob Weir's guitar playing. But he has his moments, and this was one of them. I believe it, because I too had been there when Bobby did his glorious thing during "Fire on the Mountain," when Jerry and Bobby met in midair, combined into a single comet, and sailed across the sky with Bruce Hornsby gallantly clutching the tail. The show was at the Nassau Coliseum, so they must have soared across the ceiling. That moment keeps them coming back. It is why the tapers must be comprehensive, and the spinners relentlessly keep the hallways warm.

Everyone's been to a show or a theme park and heard the announcement: *No photography or recording of this show is allowed. Violators will be cruelly punished.* Well, you never heard that at a Dead show. They were making music, and music was in the air, free. If you wanted to make a tape and listen to it when you got home, more power to you. At first the taping efforts were for just a few obsessed audioheads, but it grew until in 1984, every Dead show featured a taping section in the middle of the floor, about halfway between the stage and the back of the arena where the sound was best. In that area, microphones on poles sprouted upward like beanstalks from a psychedelic garden.

I had always assumed the spinners to be beyond earthbound stuff like lust, but apparently some exploited the Dead's sensuality. This is a story told to me by Gregg Praetorius, who was my dorm neighbor in college and went on, with his wife, Pam, to have a career facilitating rock shows. When we were in school he worked for Hofstra Concerts, and was around Jerry repeatedly in 1980 and '81 as Jerry regularly played the Calderone Theater in Hempstead, New York, either with the JGB, or with Hunter. Gregg remembers a spinner at one show, a young woman twirling and writhing to the music in the back, while her girlfriend sat on the floor next to her with her outstretched arm up her dress, apparently pleasuring her. Teamwork!

Whether working as a team, or solo, for most the music alone is enough to create bliss. The resulting feeling is that we are the eyes of the world, living absolutely our own way, "do what thou wilt" hedonism governed only by the golden rule. It is what Beauchamp calls "a sort of spiritual minimalism," left uncluttered by specifics. Being a Deadhead, or a member of the Dead, is not a political choice, it is a lifestyle choice—an ethical choice, if you will. Dead audiences never start trouble, they get high and they groove. They create what Deadhead Don Posner called "a bubble of energy floating around the country." The concert itself is what Beauchamp calls "the Epicurean Garden." In this way, by creating moments of glorious happiness so strong that being nice is a prerequisite to getting inside the tent, the Dead, Beauchamp believes, have cultivated "a community based on an experimental lifestyle," making the Dead "the most successful contemporary embodiment of Epicureanism."

When the aural holograph floats up off the stage and then over the audience, it creates among the Deadheads a kind of religious fervor during which it is not uncommon for Deadheads to guess about what is happening to them and guess wrong. They think that they are part of the mind meld, that they have power, that they are pulling the strings and making the band play the way they do. In the olden days the hallucinating were apt to link their strongest visions to Christian symbols, visions of the Virgin Mary appearing in the sky, for example, and in later years there were those who saw ghosts and aliens from Mars. So if you asked Jerry about audience members who claimed to know what the Dead would play before they played it, or that they were playing the instruments for the band with their strong connection in raw consciousness, Jerry would've said, "It's just like flying saucer reports." Try to chase one down and you learn just how elusive they are.

If the wavelengths were in synch, the band could pull off some mighty slick musical feats, the very thing that attracted the ear of academics. There were no imitators. The closest band to the Dead (Phish? Hot Tuna? Gov't Mule?) isn't very much like the Dead at all. Take, for example, the nights they musically expounded upon "Playing in the Band," which is, according to Deadhead Chris

Hardman, their "Statement of Mission." They play it—a song with an odd signature, 10/4—and then wander off in the middle for several songs from the great Grateful Dead songbook, and eventually go "Space," only to return to "Playing in the Band" later in the evening, or even later in the tour. I recalled a show in which the band went deep into "Dark Star," soaring across the galaxies, and then suddenly pulled it together, delivered a dynamite Bobby cowboy song, "Me and My Uncle," and then went back into the spaciest section of "Dark Star." Maybe the whole thing really is a dream we had during an afternoon nap long ago.

"RIPPLE" IS SO ZEN

American Dead fans, who account for nearly all of them, always feel as if the band were singing to them alone. Even when the product did have non-American influences, it is doubtful that the spinners ever figured it out. For example, take the song "Ripple," which could have been translated from Japanese for all of its Asian influences. The chorus is designed to guide us toward enlightenment, a haiku (seventeen-syllable Japanese poem) in format and a Zen koan (a paradox to be meditated upon in order to give up one's reliance on reason) in content. The "ripple in still water / when there is no pebble tossed / nor wind to blow" is like the sound of one hand clapping, a thing to ponder while meditating on the deep questions of life, questions that can have no answer.

To cop a riff from R. Crumb:

"What's it all mean, Mr. Natural?"

"Don't mean shee-it," Mr. Natural says.

That's not poking fun at the notion of enlightenment. That *is* enlightenment. Mr. Natural has figured it out—perhaps while listening to "Ripple"—and he is sharing the wisdom.

As Rutgers University English professor William C. Dowling put it in his essay "'Ripple': A Minor Excursus," the poetry and song of enlightened souls "contains no ultimate secrets." There is no religious code, there is merely a "way of thinking" that allows them to "get through life in a way that is 'higher' than the blind strugglings of the unfortunate many."

Hunter is asking his own unanswerable questions when he notes that his lyrics are recorded thoughts, broken, but his, built upon the tones and meters of the music and poetry that came before, thoughts that will be heard in the form of song and sung now and in the future leading to other thoughts and other songs —hand-me-downs—and in this way he shall achieve immortality.

The influence of Zen on the lyrics of the Dead, and on the lives of the band and its followers, is not isolated to this one song. The band's catalog is carefully etched with the notion that life consists of paradoxes, unanswerable questions, and the kind notion that all will be OK. Ambiguity is not used solely as a poetic technique, but rather as an intrinsic part of the band's philosophy. Just as lyrics suffer when divided and analyzed in parts, so does existence resist being understood as anything other than a whole, a conglomerate of unknowable components working together without flaw. In "Uncle John's Band" we are warned that danger comes to the door just as "life looks like easy street." In "Playing in the Band" we are told that the man who trusts nothing knows all will turn out right.

The connection between Dead music and Zen was not supposed to be subtle. The Bay Area during the midsixties was a hotbed of Zen, which had been thrust into popular culture through the works of Beat writers Jack Kerouac and Allen Ginsburg. In 1966, the Dead played a show at the Avalon Ballroom to benefit (or "Zenefit," as it was called) the Zen Center at 300 Page Street in San Francisco, where longtime practitioners and newbies alike could meditate and listen to "dharma talks."

The connection between Dead music and Zen is not lost on the modern Deadhead, who supports the work of cover bands with names such as the Zen Tricksters and the Addled Zen Ramblers.

THEY INVENTED A
NEW FORM OF MUSIC

You couldn't call it fusion. Fusion implies a conscious melding of two or more types of music. You could listen to the Dead with a categorical ear, and say: "That's bluegrass, that's jazz, that's classical, that's rock 'n' roll, that's cowboy." But don't think for an instant that's how *they* thought of it. This isn't what the Dead did, simply because they didn't recognize the borders between types of music to begin with. They didn't fuse genres as much as crossbreed them to make them organically linked. Their mode is stylistic polyrhythmic innovation, a civilized musical argument between the musicians, sometimes an argument between two sides of the same thing, like a fugue, with a potentially ecstatic resolution that either does or doesn't resolve on any particular evening, a freewheeling house blend, a dash of magic, Wiccan without the bitter. Phil says that the band is a paradigm of something, a model of *homo gestalt*, a phrase that for some reason didn't catch on with the other band members. Point is, you throw a sponge into a bucket of water and it's going to swell up and grow. Throw a bunch of ingredients in a pot and cook it up and you've got gumbo —and the ingredients aren't all musical. Some are social, philosophical, psychological, historical, and mythical. Sure, after playing on the same bill with Miles Davis for multiple shows, mostly at the Fillmore, the sad urban cool of Miles's horn began to seep into Jerry Garcia's solos, like osmosis, but it's doubtful that it was schematic, it just happened. It was music, man—and it was beautiful. One time Jerry and the devils jammed on a rhythmic extract from Miles's *Sketches of Spain*. Afterward Jerry said, "I play a great trumpet." Phil tried to reject Miles, told himself he didn't like the breathy notes, but Miles fought his way into Phil's playlist with his musical speedball, a seemingly paradoxical combination of wired, nervous riffs and a smooth vibe.

Miles was like the Beatles in the sense that he kept finding new ways to blow your mind. He kept changing his game, stepping it up, pushing the boundaries. Late in 1970, the Dead played a four-night stand at the Fillmore West, with Miles and a brand new band promoting his new record *Bitches Brew*.

Some saw it as the birth of something brand new, fusion jazz, and of course the Dead soaked it up. Miles was simply coming at it from the other direction. The Dead had been doing their version of it for five years already. There is an argument that fusion jazz was born the day Phil Lesh joined The Warlocks and explained that sometimes magical things happen when a band plays not as they have rehearsed to play, but rather by finding a groove and ad-libbing. The notion might have crashed and burned during early gigs in pizza parlors, where audiences and bosses alike told them to cut out the noise, but for the tenacity of these musicians who forged on until they found their audience, freshly dosed, all receivers open, at the first acid tests.

CONCERT SOUND AT
A WHOLE NEW LEVEL

This was mostly Owsley's doing: Augustus Owsley Stanley III, a brilliant lunatic rich kid from back East. Owsley was the grandson of a Kentucky senator, nicknamed "Bear" and best known for his manufacturing and distributing ultrapure acid early in the game, say '64, '65. It was he who supplied the drugs for the first acid tests, group experiences for acid-eaters organized by best-selling author Ken Kesey (*One Flew Over the Cuckoo's Nest*) and written about by Tom Wolfe in his book *The Electric Kool-Aid Acid Test*. We'll discuss that much more later. Owsley's effect on concert sound started when he recorded the Dead's shows not by standing in front of the stage with a microphone in his hand, but by plugging his recorder directly into the soundboard. The Dead were still in the acid-test phase, playing exclusively for Kesey's parties, when Phil Lesh asked Owsley to be their soundman. Instant revolution. Owsley, tripping perpetually, grabbed some speakers and turned them around so they were facing the musicians, who up until then had a difficult time hearing themselves, thus inventing stage monitors. (Although it should be noted that Bill Hanley, sound engineer for the Buffalo Springfield, claims that Neil Young originally came up with the idea. Since the Grateful Dead and the Buffalo Springfield frequently shared the same bill, we may be forced to give co-credit.) Before this, bands plugged their instruments into amplifiers connected to single-channel speakers. Mono! Owsley, on his own tab (so to speak), rewired the system so Dead shows were in stereo. Bear purchased a Voice of the Theatre system, an ugly hi-fi with a cabinet on the bottom with a fifteen-inch speaker inside, a speaker Bear likened in size to a dorm-room refrigerator. There was a small horn on top, a four-inch driver, and it produced a (for the time) tight sound. Improvements were quick in coming. For a while, Bear's stereo was the band PA.

Owsley was the first guy who stepped back from the scene a little bit, tried to put a little perspective on the big party that was going on, and he decided the Dead had a chance to be really good. He was the band's first optimist, and it was from him they learned the importance of *quality*, playing well, and getting better. Bear's generous financial backing and sound-equipment expertise allowed the band the freedom to become the Grateful Dead. They should play better and he would see to it that they sounded better when they did it. By the end of 1966, the Dead were playing through four huge Altec Voice of the Theatre A7 speakers powered by four McIntosh 240 stereo tube amplifiers. Every year the Dead's sound system grew larger; by 1974 they were blasting arenas with their "Wall of Sound," not a Phil Spector production technique, but a forty-foot-high mountain of 604 speakers, with 55 McIntosh 2300s, requiring 26,400 watts of power. Sure, the Beatles were the first band to play a baseball stadium, but no one *heard* them. Here was a system that could pull complaints from another state. (Eventually, the Dead had to scale back because their wall was too difficult to set up, dismantle, and get to the next show.) Bear's deep brain and pockets got the Dead through the period when they generated little or no income. He gave them opportunities they wouldn't have otherwise seen, but in the long run he wanted a level of control that the free spirits of the band and crew couldn't put up with indefinitely.

THEY PLAYED THE PYRAMIDS

The Pyramids and the Great Sphinx at Giza, Egypt, were something like 4,500 years old when the Grateful Dead played there on September 15, 16, and 17, 1978. To make the show even further in tune with eternity and infinity, a lunar eclipse took place as they played, the full moon darkened by the passing shadow of the earth.

Getting there was a miracle. The Middle East had been of interest to the Dead for years. *Blues for Allah* (1975) was a eulogy to Saudi Arabia's King Faisal, a Dead fan who was assassinated by his nephew. But the idea to go there to play leaped forth one night when Mickey and Phil were talking. The original concept was, "Let's get Bill Graham to take us to see the pyramids." They were so excited they went to his house and woke him up with a lot of racket and asked if they could go to Egypt. Graham said no. The band's manager at the time was Richard "Zippy" Loren, and they asked him next. Zippy said, "You guys are nuts. There's a war going on." The idea didn't go away. The Dead decided to send themselves to Egypt, and once they made that decision Bill Graham became envious and bought a ticket to come along. How could he pass up the longest, strangest trip of all?

There was a thick forest of red tape to get through. Some of the musicians had pasts, including drug busts and sundry infractions a modern theocratic dictatorship might frown upon, that complicated the acquisition of passports and visas, and the Middle East was embroiled in its usual political tensions. So, just the fact that the Dead arrived on the site, plugged in, and were ready to rock 'n' roll was a major victory. To make arrangements Phil Lesh had to put on a suit and tie (dark blue, Dunhill of New York, OMG, it burns!) and travel to Egypt in advance to convince the local leaders that a Dead concert was an excellent idea and the chances of something going really wrong were extremely slim. He pulled it off. Their record label at the time, Arista, refused to finance the trip, so the Dead paid for it out of their own pockets. They brought along recording and video equipment with the idea of putting out a movie and an album from the show, but afterward were disappointed in their performance and decided to table the tape. The Pyramids show wasn't made publicly available until many years later, as the CD/DVD *Rocking the Cradle: Egypt 1978*. The show was a little bit lackluster. Bill had a broken arm and drummed one-handed, and it wasn't like the band had Egyptian fans. Sure, there were some groovy Bedouins, but the audience was so small that wherever you looked you saw Deadhead and basketball Hall of Famer Bill Walton swaying on his crutches, which the seven-footer used because of one of a series of foot injuries that would shorten his career. So it seemed to the band like they were not as much playing at the Pyramids, but to them, and the energy flagged. Bobby tried to find the silver lining, sure the audience was made up of several hundred Deadheads who followed the band there, and (he said) a few thousand locals who had never heard rock 'n' roll music before. He thought they caught on quick, and suggested this was because rock was part African, as evidenced by the strong connection between Nubian rhythms and Bo Diddley. Oooooookay. The show didn't suck, but it didn't crackle with energy either. Keith in particular was somnambulant. (Taking Valium because no heroin was available?) Both the piano and the pianist were out of tune. Another problem was they didn't use their own sound system but rather one they'd borrowed from the Who. The recording, however, is excellent, done by Betty Cantor-Jackson using the best technology available at the time, twenty-four-track reels. It's the very fact that it ever took place at all that blows minds. They pulled it off. In celebration Jerry stuck around and watched the sunrise. They played the fucking Pyramids, man. A close second for most cosmic thing ever was the time the Dead were playing at a gig in Oregon at the precise moment that nearby Mount St. Helens erupted. So they checked it down to the second to see what song they were playing and it was, wouldn't you know it, "Fire on the Mountain."

9

THEIR INSTRUMENTS WERE
CUSTOM-MADE

The Dead's instruments were made by Alembic,* a Santa Rosa,
California, guitar laboratory run by Ron and Susan Wickersham,
former Dead sound technicians, in other words, wizards. Ron
came to the Dead as a former Ampex engineer, whose early claim
to fame was his invention of the mike splitter, which allowed a
system to deliver near-perfect sound simultaneously to the public-
address system and the record inputs. Ron started Alembic with
Bear and fellow guitar-maker Rick Turner. When making Dead
instruments, Sue chooses the exotic woods and Ron constructs
the instruments. The original concept was to get the sound purely
from the Dead's hands to the audience's ears with as few obstacles
between as possible. No surprise, the idea for Alembic was Owsley's, and he handpicked the Wickershams to man (and woman)
the mission. It's ironic that most musicians want forgiveness,
to disguise, enhance, and homogenize their sound, whereas the
Dead wanted the audience to hear the precise truth, sonic warts
and all. Ron has dealt with many musicians and found the Dead
different in that they wanted to be hip to how things work, under-

---

*An *alembic* is the pair of sealed vessels connected by a tube within which
alchemical processes take place. Originally *alembic* meant just the lid of the
vessel, where the tube attaches, but has come to mean the entire mechanism.
In addition to turning lead into gold, the machine is also, perhaps not coinciden-
tally, a key part of a moonshine still.

stand the technology, and always be willing to try something new. One of the first instruments Alembic made for the band was Phil's Guild Starfire bass, which he called "Big Red" because of its size and color. In an attempt to keep the instrument's tone absolutely consistent throughout its tonal range, Big Red had LEDs in the neck and touch-sensitive switches so that each time Phil fretted a note it would close a circuit and send a signal to an outboard filter that would locate and transmit the precise center of the tone. The problem was the instrument was too complex and frequently broke down, so much so that Phil likened it to that snazzy sports car a guy loves until it spends most of its time in the shop under repair.

Back when Ron was working sound at Dead shows he used military-grade switches and components that were radiation-resistant for use in outer space. At first he took preexisting instruments and tricked them out, a process that evolved into creating his own custom instruments. When the Wickershams talk shop they discuss things like frequency-specific wood recipes. In this way they are part of a long tradition of luthiers.

These days, 2014, they are still making six-string basses for Phil Lesh, but now the specifications include "please make it lighter," so the seventy-five-year-old Lesh can hold it for long stretches without getting tired. They also added ebony to the neck as a tonal anchor to smooth out Phil's treks into ultrahigh frequencies (a frequency-specific wood recipe). Much of the body is made of burled Mexican cocobolo with abalone inlays. Price tag: $18,500.

Pig played a battered Vox electric piano, with a tubular metal stand and a persistent tendency to wobble, no matter how level the stage, like that round café table with the book of matches shoved under one leg. That was the setup until the summer of 1968 when he replaced it with a major upgrade, maybe too much of a change. The new keyboard was a Hammond B-3, the Cadillac of rock organs, with two Leslie speakers, with multiple keyboards, and wooden organ pedals. Pig, who once could set up and break down his instrument all by himself, was now standing behind a set of keyboards that needed the whole crew to set up. It took him forever to learn how to play it.

Longtime Dead equipment manager Steve Parish remembers that Jerry treated his guitars the way a small boy treats his baseball glove. "He slept with them," Parish said. Jerry had somewhere in the neighborhood of twenty-five guitars, but most of the time he only played three of them, all custom-built.

In early 1968 Jerry was playing a gold-top Les Paul with P90 single-coil pickups, through three Twin Reverbs, two Fender 4-by-12 cabinets with JBL D120 speakers. That summer he switched to a black Gibson Les Paul. In 1969, he switched to a Gibson SG with a Vox Crybaby wah-wah pedal, a sound made famous on the album *Live/Dead*, which for many of us was our first taste of what a Grateful Dead show was like. In 1970, when the Dead made their big move (discussed in detail in chapter 26), Jerry played a 1963 sunburst Fender Stratocaster with a Brazilian rosewood fingerboard. On *Workingman's Dead* and *American Beauty*, he played a Martin D-18 and a ZB pedal steel. In 1971 he played a sunburst Les Paul, and in the spring of that year he played his first custom-made Alembic. For a brief period (May), he played a natural-finish '57 Fender Strat that was a gift from Graham Nash, but by the summer had switched to a Gibson Les Paul TV (a rare version of the late '50s Les Paul Jr. in bright yellow, made to show up on black-and-white television). Soon thereafter Jerry proclaimed Gibson Les Pauls "boring" and moved on to a Strat, more challenge. Jerry went through a phase where his head was very techy and he got into tinkering with his guitars, at one point installing his own effects loop, his own idea. This enabled Jerry to use effects (such as fuzz, flange, wah-wah, delay, reverb, and so on) between the preamp and power sections of an amplifier, rather than running the effects directly into the front of the amp. This allowed the tone and response to remain constant even when the guitar's volume output varied. It should be noted that Jerry continued to use the Graham Nash guitar through 1973, identifiable in photos because he put an alligator sticker on it. In May 1973 Doug Irwin built him a guitar (Irwin 001), which cost $1,500 and which Jerry called "Wolf." It had a maple neck, a twenty-four-fret ebony fingerboard, and a blonde body made of "quilted" western maple.

The other techy in the band, Phil, had a bass in 1973 that, in an almost absurd example of state of the art, was quadrophonic, that is, each string had separate access to the sound system.

It should be mentioned here that Jerry was not collecting guitars. When he got a new one, he often gave the old one away. The first Doug Irwin custom guitar was given to Ram Rod, head of the road crew. In 1975 Jerry decided he wasn't satisfied with any commercially available guitars. For a while he played a Travis Beam TB500 built by John Cutler, then returned to Wolf, which had been modified to Jerry's specs by Doug Irwin. It now had a coil-and-effects loop. Irwin also pulled off the Wolf sticker and had the image inlaid into the guitar. From 1979 until 1990 Jerry played "Tiger," which was the guitar that looked most familiar to Dead fans who came out of the second big baby boom. According to legend, Tiger took seven years to build; it had an ebony fingerboard on a maple neck, an arched cocobolo top and back, a vermilion neck and body striping. It had a DiMarzio SDS-1 single coil and two DiMarzio 2 humbuckers. It was Jerry's heaviest guitar at 13½ pounds. In 1990 Irwin sold Jerry "Rosebud," an $11,000 guitar with MIDI controls built in. In 1993 Jerry's next guitar arrived in the mail, built by Stephen Cripe, a Florida woodworker who was a veteran of making custom interiors for European yachts. The body was carved out of a piece of East Indian rosewood recycled from a nineteenth-century Asian opium bed. The guitar had a tonal accuracy on the high end that allowed Jerry to play notes he had long avoided. Jerry called it "Lightning Bolt." Cripe's hobby, by the way, was making fireworks, and he died in 1996 when his shed exploded. Jerry played Lightning Bolt till the end—although for his final concert at Soldier Field he started the show with Rosebud, but it broke down, and he finished the show with Tiger, just for old time's sake.

10

PIGPEN SANG THE BLUES

There is one fact about the Dead that startles me more than any other: Ron McKernan died at age twenty-seven. What? Twenty-seven? Not only did Pigpen look and sound older than he was, he died of an old man's disease. His liver was going and his stomach lining gave out. The amazing thing wasn't that he drank himself to death. That shit happened every day. It was how fast he did it. He died at the same age as Brian Jones, Jimi Hendrix, Janis Joplin, Jim Morrison, Kurt Cobain, and Amy Winehouse, other members of what the Internet has taken to calling "The 27 Club." And he did it with booze. The band stuck with him until the end. When he was extremely ill and his liver was full of holes and his stomach was perforated, they all gave him pints of blood. Twenty-seven years old: Almost impossible to believe.

Deadheads under sixty probably know of Pigpen only on record. We were five years into the Keith and Donna era before I signed on. When Pigpen was at his peak I was a kid wondering what the hell an age of aquariums was. Older fans know that once upon a time the Dead appeared to be Pigpen's band. He was the scariest one, looked like a biker, yet if someone fell asleep on the couch he was the one who covered them with a blanket. His name, according to Phil, came from his "funky approach to life and sanitation." Phil says Pig wore the same leather vest every day that he knew him. It was his idea to play "electric blues" and form the

Warlocks. The earliest long jams were Pigpen songs, as he was the original lead singer on the Dead's cover of "Good Lovin'," "Hard to Handle," a leering and lecheous version of Sonny Boy Williamson's "Good Morning Little School Girl," Howlin' Wolf's "Smokestack Lightning," and "Hurts Me Too." His versions of "Turn on Your Lovelight" took up entire album sides and were the climax of live Dead shows. "In the Midnight Hour," the Wilson Pickett hit, was the first song the Dead ever made last forty-five minutes. An early photo of Pigpen and Jorma shows two musicians who dig the blues; they are the same age, yet Jorma looks like Pigpen's son. Whatever aged Pigpen happened early, and his lifelong love of alcohol and barbeque merely continued the process. Pigpen was a greasy young white man who sounded like a sixty-five-year-old black man. When he was still strong—his health problems started in 1970, when he was twenty-four—he helped balance the Dead. During the early days when the band could have experimented themselves into obscurity, he kept them rooted in the blues, got the fans up on their feet and gave them something they could dance to, with his organ, harmonica, and been-around-the-block-*twice* voice: "Been balling a shiny black steel jackhammer / been chipping up rocks for the great highway." It was so genuine to the bone that as a kid, I just assumed it was autobiography. Pigpen was born in San Bruno, California, but identified with black music. His dad, Phil, was a Bay Area R & B deejay and boogie-woogie piano player, so Pig learned to love Lightnin' Hopkins and his ilk before he could walk. That love never left him but, as he weakened, as his eyes yellowed and his gastrointestinal woes magnified, he started losing the musical-direction battle to Jerry and the others.

Mickey Hart came in through Billy, probably the only way he could've come in. Bill and Mickey met at the Fillmore during a Count Basie concert; Mickey was good friends with Basie's drummer at the time, Sonny Payne. That first night Bill and Mickey drummed together wherever they went, on cars, on garbage cans, and in hours they were the Rhythm Devils. "Drums" was performed so that Phil, Bobby, Jerry, and Pigpen could take a leak, smoke a cigarette—do whatcha gotta do—and during "Space" Bill and Mickey took five. Jerry, refreshed, would sometimes heckle from backstage, saying things on the order of: "That sound you hear is 20,000 fucking freaks simultaneously heading for the concession stand." Or, during "Space": "Oh no, it's the scary insects! Not the scary insects!" It was at the Straight Theater on Haight Street that Mickey first sat in as a second drummer. Mickey brought much-needed energy to the combo, the others having taken so many drugs that they'd become, as manager Rock Scully put it, "dangerously laid back." The energy was crackling like Frankenstein's laboratory with the storm directly overhead, and when the show ended Jerry ran (maybe walked fast) to the back of the stage to give Mickey a hug. "This is the Grateful Dead," Jerry said. Stretching the envelope, the band also took on a second keyboardist. Tom Constanten, Phil's old college roommate and collaborator —they once spent a half semester studying a single Bach fugue— was brought in to handle the more sophisticated patterns necessitated by variant musical forms with their many key changes and unusual time signatures. Most Dead essays give short shrift to TC's contributions to the Dead legend because his time in the band was so short, but according to his friend Jay Bianchi (quixotes.com), TC's contributions to the world as a human being are even more important: "TC is a great guy, kind and gracious, a timid wizard who doesn't know the power he possesses. He knows the Dead songs intimately but never assumes that he is master of anything. I never could have a bad word to say about TC. He treads lightly on the earth making sure not to disturb anything." For a nice example of Constanten's prettier work with the Dead, check out the You-Tube of the Dead on Hugh Hefner's *Playboy After Dark* TV show in 1969 performing "Mountains of the Moon." In the same clip Hef interviews Jerry, which is pretty funny.

The Dead had established a solid "we-don't-give-a-shit-how-we-look" look, they had it down perfect, and TC was in sharp contrast, a bit of a dandy, with his starched white collars, medallions, and Nehru jacket. He contributed to Dead jams not so much by what he played, but by how he prepared his piano before he played. He couldn't play without first doing something to his instrument, quarters and then half dollars resting on the strings, maybe cellophane weaving through the strings to provide a crackling noise. The TC experiment didn't last too long, not his fault, but he did throw the band out of balance. Still, the Constanten era produced some interesting material, like just about everyone's first "Dark Star" on *Live/Dead*. This version of the Dead was never going to have mass appeal, however. Phil and Tom together overloaded the weirdness end with a steady flow of accidental music while the rock end had to fight to keep up. TC left on good terms right after the New Orleans bust. He'd just gotten another gig, a musical to compose and direct, so it was a good time to move on. The whole notion of bringing in a keyboardist in the first place had been justified with the logic that it was for Pigpen's own good. Evidence suggests that Pigpen drank more on the road than he did at home. When doctors first discovered his liver was poisonously enlarged and in trouble, their advice was for him to "stop touring." He was left off the tours to support *Workingman's Dead* and *American Beauty*, even though his contributions to those albums were a key to their success. Like Syd Barrett of Pink Floyd and Brian Wilson of the Beach Boys, Pigpen learned it was hell to stay home while your band is touring. Unlike Barrett and Wilson, Pig got out the door and rejoined the group in late 1971, although in a limited capacity. As we can hear in *Europe '72*, Pigpen had been completely replaced as keyboardist by Keith Godchaux,* and came on stage only to sing his songs. The change in keyboardists altered the Dead forever. Already, the band was moving from being an electric blues band to a jazz-oriented group, and not weird antimatter jazz like Phil and TC were into, but smooth accessible stuff set to a two-drummer mega-beat. Jerry's leads, once frantic and jittery, were increasingly graceful and capable of great drama. Bobby said they were still a rock band but they created their music as a jazz band does. They played rock but from a jazz POV.

Pigpen sang great in Europe. No matter how poorly he might've been feeling, his commitment to his part of the show was full-bore. And we can see from photographs that those powerful vocals were coming out of a physical form that was a sliver of his former self. He had lost so much weight that he remained recognizable only by the greasecake of a cowboy hat that he'd worn in hundreds of photos. He performed with the Dead for the last time at the Hollywood Bowl in June of 1972; by that time his poor health was further complicated by the hepatitis A he'd picked up in Europe. That might've been a good time to quit drinking altogether, but this was a distant past when climbing on the wagon was considered a sign of weakness. He lived for another ten months. On March 8, 1973, the wine finally tore a hole in his stomach and he died of internal bleeding. Mickey said, "He *was* the blues, he lived it and he believed it, and he got caught in that web and he couldn't break out. And it killed him." Two days later the band gathered at Bobby's for the wake, and Jerry said, "Now he *knows*."

*Keith was notoriously shy, so much so that Donna Jean had to approach the band and tell them that her husband was qualified and wanted to be the new Dead keyboard player.

Pigpen is buried in Alta Mesa Memorial Park in Palo Alto. His headstone reads,

RONALD C. MCKERNAN

1945–1973

PIGPEN WAS

AND IS NOW FOREVER

ONE OF THE

GRATEFUL DEAD

11

BOBBY BROUGHT THE MUSCLE
AND THE SUNSHINE

Though no one probably thought it through, the thing the band needed most if it was going to be successful in show business was a chick magnet, a Mr. Show Biz type, a class clown, a spacey guy who was constantly getting kicked out of class because he couldn't help but be a distraction. Welcome Bob Weir. Bobby has natural stage presence, an easy banter with the crowd for between songs when a string has broken and another needs tuning. Everyone loves Jerry's haunting songs, his soaring solos and galaxy-quest noodling, but one of the reasons that there is nothing like a Grateful Dead concert is that Bob Weir sings half the songs, sings them strong, and rocks out. "One More Saturday Night," "Mexicali Blues," "Playing in the Band" (a declaration that the only way to spend your life is *your own way*), "Sugar Magnolia/Sunshine Daydream," "Jack Straw"—where would the Dead be without him? He brought the *rock* to this rock 'n' roll band, and his lyricist John Perry Barlow the light. In contrast to Robert Hunter's smoky nocturne, Barlow's words *shine*, a shaft of light, a freshness to the air brought by ocean breezes. Even the madmen in Barlow's lyrics are sunny. From well before Barlow came aboard, Jerry's songs felt like night, Bobby's like day, often a California day: Dionysus versus Apollo. So, of course, their best collaboration is "Looks Like Rain," which opens with Jerry on pedal steel, setting the tone for a crying song, à la Hank Williams. And the song could've gotten away with just that, but it grows into what Deadhead Chris Hardman calls "almost a full-blown power ballad."

Barlow met Bobby when they were kids and went to school together for a time in Colorado. He introduced the Dead to his friend Timothy Leary in 1967, but didn't become a lyricist until after a Dead show at the Capitol Theatre in Port Chester, New York, in February 1971 when Robert Hunter went off on Bobby, who always had trouble remembering lyrics anyway and felt free to change the words and improvise during shows, most egregiously, Hunter felt, during "Sugar Magnolia."

Hunter took his lyrics seriously. Not only did he think they were great, he believed them magic, delivered to him by a series of muses that came in threes, muses that were both transparent and feminine, so that each syllable he wrote was etched in stone.

Bobby didn't see it that way and sang what he felt, or if he couldn't remember, the first syllables that popped into his head, y'all. Hunter grew frustrated and told Barlow that from now on he was Bobby's lyricist.

But, Hunter warned Barlow, there would be frustration.

"Weir uses a lyricist like a whore," Hunter spat.

Since Bobby had a record contract to do a solo album, the record that would be known as *Ace*, time was a-wastin', and the new songwriting team went right to work. In the following days they wrote "Mexicali Blues," their first collaboration. Barlow says when he wrote the words he had a specific sound in mind, and, naturally, it was nothing in texture or melody like the music Bobby set the words to. Barlow says the first time he heard the song, he was stricken, a feeling shared by no one else. Luckily, the feeling wore off quickly, and Barlow got over it. Soon thereafter, they wrote "Cassidy" (about both Neal Cassady, legendary Beat and Bobby's old roommate on Ashbury Street, and Cassidy Law, newborn daughter of a pair of extended Dead family members), and "Black-

Throated Wind" (a nighttime song whose lyrics changed over the years, about a lonely hitchhiker who yearns for the daytime and a woman he left behind).

Barlow remained on as Weir's collaborator, and they fought more than Bobby and Hunter ever had. While they were writing "Feels Like a Stranger," Bobby said Barlow's words were stilted and nobody got them, so Barlow chased him around with an empty bottle of Wild Turkey. But songs nonetheless got written, like "Estimated Prophet" (the ravings of a doped-up zealot, verbalizing his stream-of-consciousness outside the stage door, burning out his eyes as if staring at the miracle of Fatima), "Hell in a Bucket" (a Dionysian homage to the nihilism of the road in which the narrator alludes with a shrug of the shoulders to intoxicated and prurient excesses worthy of eternal damnation), "The Music Never Stopped" (music as opiate), "Looks Like Rain" (about a broken heart so fresh that the departed woman's side of the bed is still warm), and "Throwing Stones" (a call for peace and brotherhood, minimizing man's disputes by looking at the world alternately in close-up and from a distance), a Barlow/Weir take on the theme of "Mountains of the Moon."

Unlike Hunter, Barlow didn't need the Dead. He was a friend of JFK Jr., a leading expert and writer on that wondrous frontier without dimensions that is the Internet. So, when the time came he stopped working with Bobby. He does still write lyrics, however, including those for the song "Desert Dawn" by the String Cheese Incident and for the Chicago jam band Mr. Blotto.

Back to Bobby, and away from Barlow, let's not forget the Dead's most clearly autobiographical tune, "Truckin'." The world is still wondering what in the world ever became of Sweet Jane. "Truckin'" was first recorded by the Dead in 1970 on *American Beauty*, and instantly became a favorite Dead tune. It rocked out, told a true story, contained the line, "What a long strange trip it's been," and worked perfectly as a metaphor for living a life full of adventure and chance despite dangers and setbacks. And I'm not just putting it around that it's a national treasure. It's official, made so by the U.S. Library of Congress in 1997. Its writing credit —Garcia, Weir, Lesh, and Hunter—is different from any other in Dead history. It was a group effort, and as of 1970 the group's autobiography. As Phil put it, "The song *defines* the band." The title comes from an R. Crumb illustration in *Zap Comix* #1 from 1968, and the music was influenced by a 1920s jazz dance. According to *Deadbase X*, the Dead played this song live 520 times. Bobby remembered all of the words during four of them. (Kidding!)

When illness diminished Pigpen's participation at Dead shows, it was Bobby who sang the blues, and did his best to fill the void.

12

ROCK SCULLY WAS
THEIR MANAGER

If you had to guess which band in history met their future manager at an acid test, multiple choice wouldn't be necessary. It was the Dead, the manager was Rock Scully, and they would have been *nowhere* without him. When the band was sitting around a disheveled room giggling or in deep discussion about the astral plane, somebody had to figure out how to get from here to there, where to stay once they got there, and how to collect the money. That was Rock.

Again, we have Owsley to thank. Stanley didn't leave it up to the Dead to make up their own minds, which was in any case not their forte. Instead, according to Rock's memoirs, Bear said, "Guys, this is Rock, he's your new manager."

The band said, "Far out."

Bobby added, "Good luck, dude."

According to no less than the *New York* freakin' *Times*, Rock's major accomplishments as Dead manager were (1) he organized their first tours, (2) renegotiated the band's first record contract, and (3) made sure they got paid up front at Woodstock. On the other side of the coin, not all of Rock's decisions were winners; it was he who said, "Hey man, I got an idea, let's have the Angels provide security at Altamont."

During the antiwar movement, the Dead played a few schools that had been shut down by striking students. They weren't all happy about it, Jerry didn't like to take sides, but they did it, clandestine out of necessity, and Rock came up with innovative ways to get the band on campus. At Columbia University, in New York City, the musicians huddled in the back of a bread truck, thinking inconspicuous thoughts as they rolled past unsuspecting protesters.

Back in the day, one of the problems the band had was communicating with straights, those square guys in the ties who always seemed to be standing between the Dead and what they wanted, whether it be a gig, a contract, or bail. Bobby says Rock had a knack on those occasions of saying the right thing. "He could let people know what we were all about without actually explaining anything." What Rock had was charm, he communicated a sweetness of nature. If he was conning someone, even if he was conning *you*—you couldn't really get angry with him because it had to be for a good cause. Rock wrote a book—that is, he spoke it and David Dalton wrote it down, called *Living with the Dead*. Afterward, Dalton called Rock "one of the world's all-time great liars."

Fun fact: Rock was his *real* name—an homage to his great-grandfather's favorite horse. He was perhaps destined for the counterculture right from the git-go, but got his freak feet wet in 1964 when he spent a month in jail for being a white guy at a civil-rights march. What the protest movement needed—and here he was blending anti-Vietnam, ban the bomb, and equality movements into one—was a soundtrack! He joined the Family Dog, a San Francisco group that promoted concerts at the Fillmore and Avalon, and that put him in the vicinity of the Dead when Owsley decided his destiny. He was so of the moment that he was *in the room*, a clothing store at the corner of (where else?) Haight and Ashbury, when *San Francisco Chronicle* columnist Herb Caen first coined the term "hippie."

Rock lasted for almost twenty years with the Dead, but it didn't end well. During the 1980s, veterans of the druggie era were figuring out, some faster than others, that there were cool drugs and uncool drugs. Everyone by that time knew someone who'd dumped acid on top of a preexisting mental condition and had to be institutionalized or otherwise had their quality of life adversely affected. People were figuring out that cocaine never once made anyone a nicer person, and that needle drugs resulted in brutal reliance and a variety of potential health problems. But those lessons could come slowly for someone in the cocoon of a traveling rock group, especially when Mountain Girl was no longer in the picture to roll up sleeves, especially when drugs loomed large in one's legend.

It was a sad day when Jerry changed ol' ladies. Mountain Girl was out, Deborah was in. Mountain Girl was the light, Deborah, with her goth all-black clothes, was dark—though Deborah reportedly once gave MG a catty smile, so MG picked her up and threw her against a door so hard that a hinge was ripped from its mooring—and Jerry reportedly took a turn for the darker with the switch. Scully was fired in 1984 for diving off the speedball* cliff. Rock pulled out of it before crashing and outlived Jerry by more than nineteen years, not succumbing until I was sitting here writing about him on December 16, 2014. In the end, it was cigarettes that got him.

---

*A speedball is a combination of injected heroin and cocaine, made infamous as the cause of comedian John Belushi's death.

THEY DIDN'T BUY INTO THE JINX

For years, folks used to say that the Dead always blew the big ones. At the Monterey Pop Festival of 1967, a concert that helped launch Jimi Hendrix, Janis Joplin, and Otis Redding into stardom, the Grateful Dead found themselves sandwiched between Jimi, who famously set his guitar on fire and prayed over it, and the Who, who smashed their instruments at the end of their set. The Dead didn't play poorly, but it was a low-key set made up of *Viola Lee Blues* and *Cold Rain and Snow*. The audience was also distracted by a wildfire rumor when the Dead took the stage that the Beatles were there and were going to play next, which of course didn't happen. Peter Tork came on stage during the Dead's set and *announced* that the Beatles weren't on the bill. As Jerry said, "No one even remembers we were there." Their Monterey anonymity was sealed when they—suspicious of money people—refused to sign a release form before taking the stage that would have allowed their performance to be part of the subsequent documentary film.

At Woodstock, two years later, they again refused to sign the contract that would have allowed them to be part of the movie. Trouble began right off. Rock Scully and the road crew were loading the Dead's equipment onto a forty-foot turntable onstage when the platform collapsed. The Dead have always held their road crew in higher esteem than most bands, allowing roadies votes in band elections. Part of this is natural respect of a fair-minded band, but there is also a nod to the fact that it's harder to move the Dead from one show to another than it is to move, say, Three Dog Night. The Dead's stage setup was not only state of the art, but built and designed by mad scientists, so repairing it when it fizzled and smoked took guys with a special set of troubleshooting skills. At Woodstock, with the platform broken, the band's stuff had to be carried out onto the stage by hand, which took forever. The festival's crew was told to stand down, as the band would only allow Owsley to rewire the stage for their set. More delay, as tasks that had grown routine during the course of the event became, "Where's the plug for this?" No matter how Bear configured it, the band was getting shocks off of the equipment. While this was going on, there were frightening announcements (which do appear on the soundtrack and in the movie) warning people to lay off the brown acid and get off the scaffolding. At one point the band thought they were set to play when the speakers began to pick up aviation communications from the busy helicopter traffic: "Squawk, roger wilco, squawk." Just as the band finally came on stage, the sky darkened and the mother of thunderstorms struck. The wind was whipping, the sky opened up. There were sheets of rain, everyone was soaked. The giant cloth screen the crew put up for the Dead's light show turned into a sail and the stage began to slide in the mud. Things were blowing around and there was the serious possibility that they'd be electrocuted by their instruments and die.

Dead roadie Steve Parish once said, "Electricity is a strange thing. . . . It likes to mess with people." It liked to mess with the Dead at Woodstock. The band had *finally* started their first song, "St. Stephen," when a crazy guy jumped up on the stage and began to throw tabs of acid into the crowd. It turned out to be purple acid—but it looked brown, and everyone knew the brown acid was bad, so that caused acute anxiety and stopped the show for a while.

Jerry said later that the shaky performance was at least partially his fault. He was high and saw blue balls of electricity bouncing across the stage. The ball might've been real. Bobby said it came from him. He touched his guitar and his microphone at the same time and a baseball-sized spark lifted him off his feet and threw him eight feet back into his amplifier. Jerry remembered trying to concentrate on which notes to play while listening to genuinely panicky voices screaming, "The stage is collapsing!"

After "St. Stephen," they made attempts to play "Mama Tried," "Dark Star," and "High Time." They finished with "Turn on Your Love Light," with Pigpen pretty much doing his rap a cappella.

Always one to look at the bright side of the street, Jerry said that, other than their set, he had a pretty good time at Woodstock.

They never made it onto the stage at the Altamont Speedway Free Festival. Refused to play. Just as well. Bad crank and prima donna Stones had everyone mean. Later on, there was some regret. Maybe they should've played, maybe it would've been different. The Dead could smooth out a biker like a hypnotic female voice in an opium den. Maybe not. The Stones made the crowd wait and wait until dark, so their set would look better in the documentary film they were making, and violence in front of the stage plagued the Stones set from the start, culminating in a guy pulling a gun and then being stabbed to death by a biker. Maybe the reality of Altamont was locked in as atavistic, a human experiment with nothing nice to say about humanity, as in *Lord of the Flies*. Afterward, most folks blamed the Stones for Altamont, but some blamed the Dead—most significantly Ralph J. Gleason, founder of *Rolling Stone*, writing in the *San Francisco Chronicle*—and Hunter answered back, said one way or another *this darkness got to give*.

At the Summer Jam festival at the Watkins Glen Grand Prix Raceway in Watkins Glen, New York, in 1973, the biggest of them all, with an estimated 600,000 in attendance, the Dead played twice, once as part of the regularly scheduled event (which also featured the Allman Brothers Band and the Band), and once on the day before. Because of the legendary traffic jams before Woodstock, and Watkins Glen's similar narrow country access routes, so many folks showed up early that the Dead's sound check grew into a two-set show. It was the Band that had trouble with a rainstorm. So, it might seem that the dark cloud over the Dead's head was gone. Unfortunately, however, the festival was marred by a couple of deeply disturbing incidents. A skydiver named Willard Smith planned to freak the crowd out by parachuting into the show with two flares in his hands. Unfortunately he accidentally set his body suit on fire, became engulfed in flames, and was dead before he hit the ground. And, although no one knew it at the time, two Brooklyn teenagers—Mitchel Weiser, age sixteen, and his girlfriend, Bonita "Bonnie" Bickwit—who were hitchhiking to the concert didn't arrive and were never seen again.

For the Dead, it wasn't a big win. The sound-check show before about 50,000 was so far superior to the real show before 600,000 that a portion of that was the only part put on record.* Remember, they were the only band there that was also at Altamont (though the Band had also been at Woodstock). Looking out over a city of hippies must have spurred some interesting flashbacks, and it affected the music. It didn't help that overnight rain, combined with summer sun, pushed the humidity until their speakers (and everything else) was soggy. The musicians were listless, some thought tentative, like they were afraid of getting the crowd too rowdy.

When the three bands had all completed their sets, musicians from all three bands came out on stage for a show-ending jam.

---

*Unlike Monterey and Woodstock, at least some of the Dead's performance at Watkins Glen is available. An eighteen-minute jam from the sound-check show is included in the boxed set known as *So Many Roads (1965–1995)*, released in 1999.

Jerry had apparently altered his metabolism in some way since he was last on stage. He was bouncing around and all smiles, looking forward to trading licks with the likes of Dickey Betts and Robbie Robertson. It didn't go that well. They started a rocking jam, Jerry took a tentative and meandering lead, and Dickey promptly buried him.

The icy jinx first began to melt in 1977 when the Dead played their first big gig in the East at Englishtown, New Jersey. Though the vocalists had unusual trouble (even for them) remembering the lyrics to their songs, the band played two full sets and an encore, played well, and everyone went home happy. Promoters were careful to keep unticketed fans out, and the event was deemed a success. *Much* more about Englishtown later.

That snakebit feeling, however, returned in 1978 when the Dead went to Egypt to play the Pyramids and, half a world away from their favorite "pharmacy," gave a lackluster performance.

Point is, there was plenty of reason to feel snakebit whenever a "big" show approached, but they didn't let it bring them down. When they got the gig to play Philadelphia for the Fourth of July in 1989, there were all sorts of things that could've gone wrong. The concert was to be held in the soon-to-be-condemned JFK Stadium before more than 100,000 people. It was a facility that had often been the site of the Army-Navy football game, but it was decades past its prime, a fire hazard with cracked infrastructure and suspect plumbing. By the time the band took the stage it was a hundred degrees, and there was ankle-deep water in the ladies' rooms. So what did the Dead do? They gave one of their greatest shows ever. They didn't shrink from the heat, but used it. The heat became part of the music. Listen to "Ramble On Rose" and the "Scar/Fire" from that show (available on CD and as a download in the collection known as *Crimson, White & Indigo*), you can feel the radiating broil coming off the crumbling stone ruins as the band hovered above the stage, rising with the heat. The Dead show at JFK was the final event ever in that stadium. It was condemned six days later, and torn down.

14

THE BIRTH OF THE DEAD
WAS A FAMILIAL PROCESS

It happened like a Bay Area version of "Creeque Alley."* At the center is Garcia, fifth-generation San Franciscan on his opera-loving mom's side, musicianship on his Spanish dad's side. José Ramon "Joe" Garcia was an orchestra leader during the Depression—big bands and big orchestras, forty pieces, strings, a harp! He played Treasure Island, the famed site built in the Bay for the 1939 Exposition. Dad downsized at some point to four- and five-piece bands that played Dixieland jazz. So Jerry was born into a house of music, named in honor of composer Jerome Kern, who composed "Smoke Gets in Your Eyes," "Ol' Man River," and "The Way You Look Tonight," among other classics. His mom, Ruth "Bobbie" Garcia, played piano, and little Jerry took piano lessons while still in diapers. By age five Jerry was down to nine fingers, after a wood chopping accident with his brother while vacationing in the mountains, and that was that for tickling the ivories. Jerry would one day return to the keyboard as a writing tool with spectacular results. The missing finger became a thing, of course, almost a logo, and at one time the subject of much speculation. Folks liked to believe it was cut off as part of some sort of punishment or initiation, or to dodge military service, to which Phil took great delight

* "Creeque Alley," written by John and Michele Phillips, was a 1967 hit single that told the story of the birth of the Mamas and the Papas. You've heard it: "John and Michi were gettin' kind of itchy just to leave the folk music behind."

in saying, "Nope, it was axe-idental!" Jerry's dad owned a bar down by the docks of the city and played clarinet, sax, reeds, and wood-winds in some of the same San Francisco jazz clubs that his son would later haunt. But Jerry's dad drowned with Jerry watching when Jerry was five, so everything after that has to be examined through a post-traumatic stress lens. Mom took over the water-front saloon next to the merchant marine union hall. Jerry spent a lot of time looking at the publicity shots of his old man, and wondering what it's like to be in a band. When Jerry was fifteen he turned on the radio and he couldn't believe what he heard at all; he gets an accordion for his fifteenth birthday, simultaneously gets a hankering to play guitar, no, electric guitar, that's why he goes for that rock 'n' roll music, so he takes his accordion to a pawn shop and trades it in for a Danelectro axe, a coffin-shaped case, and the world's smallest amplifier. He's on top of the world, happiest day ever. Later, Jerry says that's the day he left the "straight world," never to return. Now what? He's got no one to teach him to play, no books. So he tries to do it by ear, doesn't get very far, early prog-ress inhibited by a steady flow of experts all telling Jerry how to incorrectly tune the thing. He's only made a little progress when he finds a kid at school that knows the correct way to tune a guitar —and three chords. It's all just fooling around until he's eighteen and hears bluegrass, Earl Scruggs and his five-string banjo, and Jerry's got a new obsession. Jerry tries the army for nine months, a bad fit, he's discharged for crummy conduct, and so finds him-self in a Palo Alto coffee shop near the Stanford campus listening to folk music when in walks twenty-year-old Robert Hunter, born in San Luis Obispo where he became stepson to a literary editor and began writing seriously while still in grade school. Jerry Garcia and Robert Hunter have a lot in common. They're both living out of their cars and hungry, so they start a folk act, first gig five bucks apiece. Jerry can play the banjo like nobody's business and Hunter switches back and forth between a standup bass and a mandolin and sings a little. They're the Tub Thumpers.

Also hanging around are (future Jefferson Airplane and Hot Tuna lead guitarist) Jorma Kaukonen and Janis Joplin from Texas, and a friend named Ron "Pigpen" McKernan who doesn't bathe and has looked forty since he turned fifteen. Pigpen digs blues and his dad is an R & B deejay nicknamed "Cool Breeze." Jerry and Pig join a band called the Zodiacs, and they play strip joints, which pays shit but has fringe benefits.

Hunter and Jerry do their folkie thing in a Menlo Park shingle house called the Chateau, sort of a rooming house/hangout for young creative types. David Nelson, later of the New Riders of the Purple Sage, joins in with Hunter and Jerry and they call themselves the Wildwood Boys with Jerry on banjo. One day during the autumn of 1959 Jerry and Hunter are in the Chateau when in wanders Phil, a jazz-band vet from Berkeley who's working as an engineer at a radio station. Phil was a childhood prodigy, first on the violin (he played second fiddle in the Young People's Symphony Orchestra, playing Wagner's *Die Meistersinger von Nürnberg* and Franz Schubert's *Unfinished Symphony*), and then the trumpet, becoming lead trumpet player in his high school band when only a freshman, and eventually second trumpet for the Oakland Symphony Orchestra, playing behind only his trumpet teacher. Phil, like Jerry, has music in his blood, all kinds of music, music that brightened his earliest memories and eased his pubescent passage, music that other people can't even hear because they are so out of tune with the possibilities. Phil's dad Frank played the piano and could exuberantly belt out pop songs by ear. Dad also played clarinet in a band around Ohio, and his grandmother was a serious music freak, classical, opera. Grandma Bobbie took Phil's mother to the opera or the philharmonic when she was a child, and Phil remembers those types of music from his own childhood, listen-

ing to fantastic radio broadcasts: opera and the New York Philharmonic on Saturday nights and Sunday mornings. He remembers
the first time he listened to music with his grandma, she woke him
up and asked him if he wanted to get up and listen, and it was magical. She told him that it was some of the best music ever written,
ever performed. She said it was Johannes Brahms. Another thing
Phil inherited from his dad was an interest in and the ability to
visualize the inner workings of machines. Now his friend Jerry is
playing the banjo and Phil can't believe his ears, the riffs, the ideas,
they are pouring like liquid over one another until they're splash-
ing up over his shoes. Phil noticed right away that people "deferred
subtly" to Jerry, acknowledged him as a spokesman, an expert on
everything that was cool and far out. Jerry had a guru vibe, but he
was so open-minded that Phil couldn't find anything despicable in
it. Phil worked for KPFA, an ultra-alternative radio station. There
he is engineer for the folk music show called *The Midnight Special*.
He makes a tape of Jerry playing banjo (using Tom Constanten's
Wollensak reel-to-reel tape recorder), has no trouble convinc-
ing his boss that Jerry was show-worthy, and Jerry plays his first
ninety-minute radio gig: "'The Long Black Veil' and Other Ballads,
an Evening with Jerry Garcia." Jerry meets his first wife in a cutesy
scene right out of a bad romance novel: he's schlepping his guitar
across the ranch-like Stanford campus and rich girl Sara's riding
a bike, so he hitches a ride and hangs on for a few years, teaming
up with her as a pair of ban-the-bomb folkies who walk out on
Dylan when he plugs in at the 1963 Monterey Pop Festival, a full
two years before it was *cool* to walk out on a plugged-in Dylan at
the Newport Folk Festival. Jerry and Dylan of course later made
amends, while Jerry and Sara eventually split, Sara taking daughter Heather with her, and latching on to the Pranksters. Jerry's
next ol' lady (Mountain Girl) came out of the Pranksters' ranks, so
it was like a trade.

Meanwhile, Phil makes the trip from bass-caterpillar to bass-butterfly at warp speed, and says in his book *Searching for the Sound*, "Whoa, most musicians start out playing pop, then move on to blues, then jazz, then classical. I did it backwards."

Mickey remembered a time when Hunter had a room above the Potrero Theater on Potrero Street, the same theater in which the Dead had a rehearsal space and Mickey would go to visit him there. Mickey recalled for David Gans, "That's when he was drinking. We'd push the door open and he'd be there on the floor with wine bottles. He was taking speed and drinking wine—and writing all this beautiful stuff."

Not long thereafter, Hunter went away for a while to kick a bad speed jones, try Scientology, join the National Guard and freak himself out while helping to bust up the Watts riots. Counterintuitively, he explodes with creativity, writing in quick succession "St. Stephen," "China Cat Sunflower," and "Alligator."

With "China Cat Sunflower" Hunter felt the first twinge of inspiration when he was in Mexico, overlooking Lake Chapala, and the words didn't come to him, just the feline-feet-across-a-soft-footstool rhythm that was key to its seductive nature. In his vision that day the cat was real, sitting on his chest as they transported together to Neptune. Hunter, born Robert Burns and then adopted by his stepdad, is a full-fledged Scot, and channels his namesake when he writes his most emotional verse.

Back in Palo Alto, New Year's Eve 1963, here comes rich-kid Bobby, who's the son of a single mom who put him up for adoption, and the adopted son of a successful engineer, Fred Weir, and his homemaker wife, Eleanor. Weir, hopelessly dyslexic and eight-times expelled, claims to be sixteen but looks twelve, says he's just coming off a stint as a cowboy, ran away from home, got a job on a ranch, but it was too much work, especially since the new kid always gets the shovel. One day he realized you didn't have to be a cowboy to be a cowboy singer. Now he's trying to learn how to play his seventeen-dollar Japanese guitar. Jerry gives guitar lessons at a record store where one of the salesmen is Bill Kreutzmann, who's a solid pro-level rock 'n' roll drummer, and also gives drum lessons at the store in the evenings. Bill's dad, Big Bill, listens to the R & B radio station out of Oakland, and his mom is a dance teacher at Stanford. Bill's first experiences as a drummer are helping his mom with her dance classes. He has to grow up fast when he marries and becomes a father while still in high school. So, while Bill's in the music store trying to sell stuff, Jerry is in a back room quickly figuring out that Bobby is never going to play guitar like other people, but being an open-minded guy he finds much of the stuff that Bobby does do real interesting.

Jerry says let's start a jug band, Mother McCree's Uptown Jug Champions, and everyone says cool. Bobby gets to join because, unlike the guitar, he can really play the jug. (Jerry is never certain if Bobby can play guitar, and although he sometimes commented on the oddball charm of Bobby's rhythms, Jerry also publicly expressed embarrassment when Bobby tried to play slide on stage.)

Trouble is, Pig and his harmonica are the only things making them *legit*, and no one wants to hire a jug band—so Pig says, let's do electric blues instead. Everybody says cool.

Just then the Beatles hit, and there's a whole new template. Jerry trades in his Danelectro for a red Guild Starfire, his main axe until 1967. Bobby's got himself a Gretsch Country Gentleman strapped on and he's ready to go. No more haircuts (except for Bill), and now they're the Warlocks: Bobby, Jerry, Pig, Bill, and bass player Dana Morgan—whose equipment they're using, and whose dad is Jerry and Bill's boss and owner of their music store/rehearsal space.

Bill gets to be the manager because he's the groomed straight guy. They play three gigs at Magoo's Pizza in Menlo Park. Schooled in a potpourri of musical traditions, most of which aren't rock 'n' roll, that's nonetheless what they play: Kinks, Stones, Chuck Berry. Luckily Bill knows how to rock, and his beat gets the kids to dance. First gig, no one's there. Second gig, a few stragglers. Third gig, word's gotten round, four hundred schoolkids pack the place.

Sticking up out of the crowd like a sunflower among dandelions, because he's tall and has a blond Beatle/Fauntleroy haircut, is Phil. He thinks it's a riot that Jerry and Pigpen are in a band together, because he'd always associated them in his mind even when he knew them separately. That was because they not only looked like each other, Phil thought, but because both resembled the wildly progressive late nineteenth- and early twentieth-century classical composer, Claude Debussy. Like Jerry, Phil tried the army —he'd wanted to play with the Sixth Army Band stationed in San Francisco—but was 4-F because of his eyesight. The first time Phil ever got stoned on pot, he was with his friend Bobby Peterson (co-composer of "Unbroken Chain"), and listened in the dark to Igor Stravinsky's orchestral concert work *The Rite of Spring*. "Man, you can't believe what I'm hearing," he said. Now Phil's got a job at the post office and an apartment in Haight-Ashbury. Jerry digs Phil's musical sensibilities, they'd rapped for hours, and wants him in the band—the music store owner's kid isn't cutting it, Jerry has to tell him which notes to play, and they need a bass player. Phil says I don't play bass, and Jerry says, that's OK, you'll learn. Here's a quote: "By god, I'll give it a try," Phil says, and promptly adds a shitload of three-staff avant-garde to the scene. The Warlocks think they look like the Beatles because of the hair, but they've missed the mark by some measure, instead appearing as a freaky mix of humans, just a little bit scary: a Mexican guy, a bespectacled string bean, a feminine-featured teen, an overweight biker, and a surly JD. They look like trouble. They would one day become high-tech, but at this point everything they bring to shows fits easily inside Billy's Dodge station wagon. Phil practices bass for four days, sticking tape on the neck to indicate frets, and goes to his first band rehearsal. The very first song Phil plays with the Warlocks is "I Know You Rider," because Phil already knows the chords, and Jerry used to do it acoustic as a folk song. All of a sudden there's a guy in the band who once wrote a symphony for four orchestras with the audience in the middle, who discusses anti-notes, who says that in the ultimate music there are no key signatures, no melodies, and who wants to make improvisation and musical conversation a group focal point. Phil's been into musical improv ever since he was a kid trying out for a high-school dance band, reading along with the music when he came to a part called "Ad Lib," which meant play something that wasn't written. The concept clearly changed his life. With Phil on board, the band can no longer use rehearsal space belonging to Dana Morgan's dad, so they move band HQ to Guitars Unlimited in Menlo Park. Eventually they would set up a long-term rehearsal space in San Francisco's oldy-moldy Potrero Theater, where the asbestos came raining down from the ceilings if the band hummed into a particular vibration. Jerry's cosmic side digs Phil, digs that his bass lines are light years beyond Jerry's ability to understand. Phil, more than any of the other musicians, plays according to mood. If he's pissed off or not feeling well, he might have a bad night (and they all have bad nights) but when Phil is down the band is likely to be down, too. Listen to the ten best Dead shows ever, and they all have something in common—Phil's on fire. People think Jerry's the musical director of the Dead because of his gift for gab, but it's a true democracy, and Phil—just like Reggie Jackson and his championship New York Yankees—is the straw that stirs the drink. The band, though tender in years, is already a perverse democracy in which the vote is almost always everyone against the guy whose idea it is. No one gets his way most of the time. It's funny that people think Jerry's in charge, or Pigpen's in charge. Pigpen got respect at least, but no one listens to Jerry. Sure, Jerry could be the powerful one when performing, but he hardly ever gets his way at band meetings. Phil did better. Even though Phil's the new guy, he's got some juice on account of he's holding down his fair share of street cred, the guy with real-life experiences that would have made the best Dead songs. He once tried to set Allen Ginsberg's *Howl* to music. At age twenty, he hitchhiked to Calgary, Alberta, looking for work in the oil fields. Turned out there was no work so he returned, getting from Spokane to Seattle by hopping a freight train. While working at the post office, he shoots meth, and makes grown bus drivers cry by driving the mail truck like it was a weapon and life one never-ending game of chicken. Not long after joining the band, Phil's bringing all of that credibility and more to his brand new and complex bass lines, which are far more melodic than most bass players play, a symptom of a musician who has become a bass player. Sometimes he's playing trumpet on the bass, sometimes violin, sometimes he's telling a reporter how much respect he has for tightwire walker Karl Wallenda who said the wire was life and all else was waiting around. Phil says that's how he feels about the band. The band is life—everything else is waiting around—a great line, as long as you don't say it to your ol' lady. Pretty soon it's not just an electric blues band, not just a rock 'n' roll band anymore. Pigpen's portion of the program remains strong, but now there's a new thing going on. It's now a *psychedelic* band, whatever that is. It's the soundtrack to the new scene, and the new scene is shaping up to be genuinely new—something wilder than the Peter, Paul and Mary crowd, just a little bit sweatier than the Kingston Trio. That scene had the relevant but well-behaved Joan Baez. This one had Grace Slick (who's singing her songs "White Rabbit" and "Somebody to Love" for a band of her siblings called the Great Society, while the Airplane was also around), Janis Joplin (a bit of a discipline problem, making her the first real female rock star) was just learning of her own power, the ability to take blues vocals to a new level, the same way *electric* guitar lifted the genre. Grace and Janis were ice, fire, and trouble—increasingly stormy with a chance of insane. The Warlocks are taking tentative treks, puddle jumps, into space (only the very closest stars) even when they are still playing straight gigs—and the youngsters who come out *hate* them for it. All the kids want is a cover band with correct hair that could rock, play "Johnny B. Goode," play "(I Can't Get No) Satisfaction," "Help." What's all this namby-pamby scale diddling? Turns out there's another band in New York called the Warlocks (they later become the Velvet Underground), so the Palo Alto Warlocks need a new name. It was such a grown-up thing to do. They had to rename the band because of potential conflicts when they recorded their first record. That kind of foresight and optimism was a major step forward for a group that previously might have ranked chicks over bread as a benefit of being a musician. The early favorite for new name is the Mythical Ethical Icicle Tricycle, but it is soon forgotten. One particularly charged evening, a night shimmering nervously, everyone's smoking dope and hanging out at Phil's when Jerry flashes on an open copy of *Funk and Wagnall's Standard Dictionary of Folklore, Mythology, and Legend*, two words juxtaposed: "Grateful" and "Dead." Jerry doesn't like it. Bobby and Bill don't like it. Phil hates it. It is too weird, too *powerful*. Nobody likes it. They start saying it out loud just to freak each other out. They all have ball-busting in common, technical crew too, and freaking guys out by saying "Grateful Dead! Grateful Dead!" becomes a zesty yet stoned ball bust. Others pick up on it, and it becomes their new name. After a while, the band comes to appreciate the name. It turns off curiosity seekers. It appeals to youngsters because parents hate it, but it *always* makes Jerry uncomfortable, queasy almost, and he refuses to be photographed in graveyards to promote the band.

15

OF THE ACID TESTS

Flash back to Jerry's old partner Robert Hunter on the Stanford campus being a human guinea pig for government experiments on a new drug called LSD. Phil has already tripped, his first listening experience on acid being Gustav Mahler's Symphony no. 6 in A minor, aka the *Tragische*, or Tragic Symphony, on the early 1960s hi-fi with the sound turned to eleven, as he conducted with the elongated gestures of a malleable maestro. Phil was already a guy who wrote music for a mime troupe, so for him the weirdness of LSD was a good fit. Now his band has just changed its name to the Grateful Dead and he's taking LSD through the eyeballs with an eyedropper, kicks in quicker that way. Lysergic acid diethylamide had been around since 1938, when the chemist Albert Hofmann synthesized it, but it would be five years (April 19, 1943) before anyone took the stuff and realized its trippy potential. Creating a psychedelic drug was not the object. The idea was to make a respiratory and circulatory stimulant. The first to trip was Hofmann himself who, when handling the drug, absorbed enough through his fingertips. Later he wrote down how he felt: "I was affected by a remarkable restlessness, combined with a slight dizziness. At home I lay down and sank into a not unpleasant intoxicated-like condition, characterized by an extremely stimulated imagination. . . . I perceived an uninterrupted stream of fantastic pictures, extraordinary shapes with intense kaleidoscopic play of colors." Far out, man. The stuff has already leaked out into the mainstream back East when Hunter sneaks some out of the hospital and gives it to the savage young Warlocks and everything goes *kablooey*. The borders between things dissolve, and the band starts to play differently. Songs get longer and louder, metamorphose into jams. Jerry says, "Whoa, man, when you're improvising cosmically each note becomes like a whole universe." Everybody else says, "Outasite." The Dead play the Chateau in Menlo Park, a couple of blocks from Ken Kesey's place. Kesey was an athlete and outdoorsman, a magician and a thespian, a pioneer psychedelic experimenter and an alpha male who'd earned credibility with both the literati and the Beats with his first novel *One Flew Over the Cuckoo's Nest* in 1962. Following the publication in 1964 of his second novel, *Sometimes a Great Notion*, Kesey bought an International Harvester school bus, called it Further, and took a group of hippie prototypes, Merry Pranksters, on the most famous cross-country tour since Kerouac. Among Kesey's Pranksters are Page Browning, Mike Hagen, and Ken Babbs—but the Prankster most important to this story is the beautiful inside and out Mountain Girl (aka Carolyn Adams), who becomes Jerry's ol' lady. The Pranksters have just gotten back from the East Coast where the acid scene is a joke, like the way acid freaks will act on future episodes of *Dragnet*. The Mellon-heir millionaire Billy Hitchcock is involved in the large-scale manufacturing of LSD on his four-thousand-acre estate near Millbrook, New York. Hitchcock has transformed his estate, which is large enough to be called a compound, into a huge LSD temple. There's a brief time when all these academic types and power-elite bullshitters are babbling about LSD's genuine universe-creating power, boasting that it reveals a new meaning to reality that's invisible to the poor slobs who haven't tripped their brains out. They've got shrinks there that are experimenting with the drug, both on themselves and on others, saying that LSD triggers an integrative experience that enhances beauty and light and causes great relaxation and hyper-euphoria. Less was said about the fact that taking LSD was, in essence, chemically induced psychosis. For a while Millbrook was the focal point of the druggie world. Looking for the party, the Pranksters showed up with Neal Cassady (of Kerouac's *On the Road* and, later, Wolfe's *The Electric Kool-Aid Acid Test*), driving the Further bus while tripping. "Hey Cassady, how can you drive when you're so stoned?" "Easy," he says. "I differentiate between reality and hallucination and drive *through* the hallucinations." Whereas Kesey's clan was into fun and mischief, the people at Millbrook took LSD seriously. They were "mapping consciousness." The entire scene began to feel very Buddhist, cool if you're into that, and the drug with which they experimented became something *sacred*. There were the usual ascetic-with-a-woody contradictions (i.e., hypocrites). It got to be a drag, and the Californians quit the place, throwing a smoke bomb over the wall on their way out, and Cassady drove into the sunset until they reached ocean.

Upon arrival at the Pacific, Kesey says, "Jerry, why don't you guys quit those straight jobs and be my house band."

Jerry says cool and there follows the dawning of Aquarius, two months of playing *nothing but acid tests*, then Avalon Ballroom dances that are like one, long, all-encompassing kaleidoscope.

While they play Kesey works the room, telling folks, "The Grateful Dead are faster than light drive!"

Sometimes the band plays great, inside each other's heads, like telepathy only real, like the band is one pulsating organism, watching light drive recede in the rearview mirror—other times they're a mess, everyone inside their own tune, getting into their own universe. When it clicks it is magic, a whole new level of consciousness. But Jerry digs it both ways: good, bad, blow the roof off the joint, or just crumble and melt in front of the audience. That's the beauty of the acid tests and such a great way for a band to develop chops because there is no pressure. The audience doesn't care if it's Ludwig Van Beethoven or bullshit, it's a happening, they just want *something* to happen. Take enough of the Owsley pure and, as he later tells David Gans, all Jerry can think is, "We're all earthlings, man. Considering the enormity of the cosmos, us earthlings ought to stick together, you know?" And no one, not even Jerry, cares who the band is. As the acid tests progress from event to event and from venue to venue, they evolve, changing from the freak-out whatever goofiness of the Pranksters into a weird rock show in which the great bulk of the entertainment is provided by loud electronic music, less of Kesey's Dr. Gestalt action and more concert-experience-event à la promoter Bill Graham. Jerry learns a trick where he can make his guitar sound like it's laughing, and that's always good for a freak-out. While playing in bars they had to *work*, there was a *boss* who pointed at his watch if they slacked, fifty minutes on, ten off, again and again—but at a test no one *really* knows what time is. Play a couple of good notes and walk off. Audience loves it. The Dead develop a side that's completely *free-form*, and they never lose it. Jerry's yearning for a way to break free of music's formality, so the acid tests are perfect. Acid tests, ha! —musical maelstroms named as sort of a mocking tribute to the government experiments, magical things are always happening (a Native American slideshow projected on the skin of a tepee, far out), everybody doses big-time, equipment writhes and squirms, music comes out of speakers that aren't even plugged in.

Kesey says, "Stay in your own movie, man."

Owsley and Kesey are self-aware as founding fathers of psychedelia, and they get into the ceremony of it, the pied-piper garb and light, but also the dark-arts dress-up fun, ceremonies stolen from the ancient fraternal secret societies, updated into San Francisco cool, like maybe they were 33rd degree members of the Tripmasons or the Ramble On Rosicrucians. Owsley had a relentless feeling that he was on the verge of eternal answers. In those early days he had trained himself to see sound, and that helped him with his innovative sound-system thinking. Bear saw the Warlocks play at an early Kesey party. He remembers the day that Mountain Girl told him the band had changed their name. The Pranksters were Grateful Dead nuts. Then Kesey got busted, faked his own suicide, and split to Mexico. Unable to face the reality of missing one of his own acid tests, Kesey came back into the country drunk and on horseback. Hippies at the test were instructed to bring transistor radios and to tune in to a particular frequency, and when they did it was Kesey broadcasting himself into the test from a nearby transmitter. The vintage Dead that the Pranksters dug was a combo of electric blues and shamanic rituals, something very old and mystical, a musical MacGuffin. Pranksters were proto-Deadheads, so free to be happy and just happy, and early Dead became a reflection of that philosophy. One time the band had a chance to get some free publicity abroad when a comically straitlaced British Broadcasting Company television crew came to an acid test to cover the scene. The trouble was, many of the testers waited for the acid to kick in and then stripped naked. The BBC tried to film the band, but every clip was rendered unusable when completely naked hippies bounced and giggled into the frame, dancing the monkey in front of the stage. One time at the Fillmore, Jerry is so stoned he stops playing in the middle of a jam and stares at the neck of his guitar with a troubled expression on his face.

"What happened?" someone later asks.

"I couldn't remember what it was," he says.

Owsley rented a house in the Watts section of Los Angeles, a troubled neighborhood known for its blight and urban desolation, and moved in his acid-making apparatus and the Grateful Dead. Owsley has the band out on the street selling LSD, turning on musicians, trying to create regular customers. In the meantime, the trip never stops. They don't even have to drop any, it's in the air, its dust covers every surface, they go to sleep and wake up tripping, all while Bear is insisting that no plant materials be consumed, that their diet must consist only of meat and milk. Armed with their new name they record a single, "Don't Ease Me In," backed with "Stealin'," on Scorpio Records (available on YouTube), with Pigpen's organ featured so heavily that they could pass for ? and the Mysterians or the Sir Douglas Quintet, and they receive their first-ever airplay when San Francisco deejay Dan Healy gives the Dead's 45 a spin, causing Tom Donahue, future innovative FM programmer, to call his old radio pal Joe Smith at Warner Bros. Records. It is happening fast now. They decide to cut a whole album (yeah!), and so book time at Coast Recording on Bush Street, where to get into the counterculture mood, they drape an American flag over Pigpen's Vox, which the studio manager treats as a criminal offense akin to treason and kicks them all out on their ear.

There was all of this talk about how great LSD is, with quasi-magical qualities and a mystical power, how it was going to change the world. What it turned out to be was a fad like the twist and Hula-Hoops.

True, like the Hula-Hoop it never really went away, as there will always be tripping as a key ingredient in your wilder coming-of-age stories. But the LSD era, the time when *acid was king*, lasted only a few years, it was made illegal on October 6, 1966 and that was the beginning of the end, and no one came out of it smarter. There's an argument that only the Grateful Dead used LSD to its fullest potential. By using it as a tool to improvise music on the same plane, they transformed themselves from a not-terribly-tight rock 'n' roll band into a psychedelic powerhouse with a sound that lives on, a phenomenon that grew and thrived decades after everything else psychedelic was gathering dust in the attic with the black light and the Peter Max posters.

Phil wrote it in his book, "Without the acid tests, we'd've been just another band."

In the fall of 1966, some of the band moved into a house at 710 Ashbury—Bobby rooms with Cassady, Phil with Jerry (very briefly, because of Jerry's seismic and truly legendary sleep-apnea snoring)—and it's a cool scene until *Time* magazine comes knocking, *Newsweek* runs a cover story, Scott MacKenzie records *that song* ("San Francisco"), and runaways start showing up in droves with empty pockets and flowers in their hair, until the consumers way outnumber the providers. Then the band gets busted and that's that. No more tests. Final exam. From now on the audiences will be judgmental, and they will want competence. It's like growing up. Besides, the Haight is *shot*. Tour buses with loud speakers drive by 710 Ashbury, a guide pointing out the *real* hippies. A bald Hollywood director, one that also played a special guest villain on the *Batman* TV show, is making a movie that uses the counterculture for comic relief. When he comes to the Dead house, scouting a location, and possibly talent, he never makes it inside as he is pelted with water balloons thrown from an upstairs window by Bobby and Mountain Girl. George Harrison comes to visit late summer '67, and the Dead see the Haight through his fresh eyes: what a mess, runaways showing up without the sense to get out of the rain, human wreckage everywhere, coke and smack available on the corner. George is appalled, the Dead see the light —time to move to the country. Jerry trades in his red Guild Starfire for a 1957 Gibson Les Paul with P90s, covers removed, and a Bigsby tailpiece. David Crosby shows up and tells the band they should get into stressed harmonies. Cool, but they aren't going to be squeezed into anybody's pigeonhole. Cassady is found dead of exposure alongside rail tracks, trying to count the number of ties between Nogales, Arizona, and San Miguel de Allende, Mexico, but before that the Summer of Love was already over, destroyed not just by autumn but by the spotlight of fame, an influx of hard drugs, a dearth of responsibility, and an overabundance of scapegoating—but the Dead plow on, as bohemian and experimental as ever. *Sgt. Pepper's Lonely Hearts Club Band* had hit that summer and forged a weird alliance between corporate-controlled pop music and a wildly independent artsy scene out of the Bay Area that would come to be known as acid rock. The most popular band in America was the Monkees, as manufactured as they come, but in the studio Micky Dolenz was starting to fiddle around with a Moog synthesizer, and is seen again and again in the Monterey Pop Festival movie having a good time with all of his fellow hippies. On the absolute other side of the coin is the Grateful Dead, one of several San Francisco acts that is musically interpreting the drug movement, mistaken by newsstand-magazine journalists for the next up-and-coming teenybopper band, bound to have a hit single any minute now. Sounds unbelievable? The proof is in the photos of a very well-behaved looking Grateful Dead posing during their studio shoot for *Teen Set* magazine. That was about the first time the band came East to see how the other half lived, and didn't take to Manhattan right away. Or maybe ever. That first visit they were afraid of New York and spent a lot of their time in their hotel. Too many people talking too fast in too much of a hurry. They knew NYC had a poetic core, but they couldn't get past the kinetics to get at it. Put the Grateful Dead on a NYC sidewalk and all those guys did was duck. So they weren't relaxed, but they did have a good run, starting in Alphabet City with a free concert in an embattled and decidedly uptight Tompkins Square Park, followed by several nights at the Café au Go Go—a very hip place for a quality rock band, a thinking man's rock band, to be heard by the right people. Franz Zappa and the Mothers of Invention played there. Just vacating the premises when the Dead arrived were those other Warlocks, the Velvet Underground, with Lou

Reed, John Cale, a German girl named Nico who sang tones in perfect ovals, and a heavy-lidded entourage of Andy Warhol types—much mascara and heroin chic. In that venue the Dead were seen at first as TV clichés, hippies from San Francisco. Did they smoke banana peels before the show? The show got off to a slow start because—shocker!—Jerry needed to tune, and tune, and tune. But over the first night, and subsequent nights, the rock intelligentsia fell under the spell, and wrote much about the Dead's patient ability to create a hypnotic sound poem. Any reference to poetry in a comment was high praise in those days as the Beats were still worshipped as gods—Kerouac, Ginsberg, and yeah, Cassady. They finished their New York run with another free concert, this one in the Great Meadow of Central Park in front of about 300 nondancing and slightly confused people. There is no hint whatsoever that these guys will one day play stadiums. The trip to New York is not a disaster, it is a learning experience, and the band eventually appreciates their NYC fans, who are so smart, but out West is where the Dead's fans are most loyal, and they know the deal: the Dead will try anything they want to try, and in exchange they agree to be whatever the audience believes them to be. Fair trade. The Dead go on their first coast-to-coast tour, playing old movie houses, and brokedown palaces of all stripes. Owsley does a year in stir, first at the Terminal Island Federal Correctional Institute in Los Angeles and then at the Lompoc Federal Penitentiary in Santa Barbara, after a late '67 raid on his acid-tabbing factory. Jerry says the Dead is a signpost warning people of dangers and detours. He says it's important to get high because out of the formlessness and chaos come new forms, and it makes you a conscious tool of the universe. Psychedelics don't give you the answers, they give you the questions. Folks who aren't turned on tend to believe that the physical visible world is all there is, whereas the turned-on dude knows that's ridiculous. "One thing I'm certain of," Jerry says. "The mind is an incredible thing and there are levels of consciousness that are way beyond what people are fooling with in day-to-day reality." Folks say Jerry is the spiritual advisor to the rock scene. "That's a crock of shit," Jerry told *Rolling Stone* magazine. "I'm just a compulsive question-answerer." But it's too late. The cat is out of the bag—Jerry is giving language to a cultural revolt—and stretching out, a little edgy, under the stars.

THE LYRICS OF ROBERT HUNTER
ARE GREAT POETRY

The lyrics of Robert Hunter can be both cosmic and poignant, transcendent and heartbreaking. They have been discussed by wide-eyed fans (most notably musician, writer, record producer, and Deadhead, David Gans) in the same breath as the poetry of T. S. Eliot, William Carlos Williams, Walt Whitman, and Dylan Thomas. And there are points (most likely made up of homage) at which comparisons to the greats can be made: Check out the opening lines of "Dark Star" ("Shall we go, / you and I / while we can / Through / the transitive nightfall / of diamonds?") and T. S. Eliot's "The Love Song of J. Alfred Prufrock" (Let us go then, you and I, / When the evening is spread out against the sky / Like a patient etherized upon a table"). The Hunter lyrics go on to hypothesize a new universe growing out of a collapsed star.

But for me, the best of Hunter's work compares better to the well-crafted symbolism of John Steinbeck and the spare, wholly masculine word-paintings of Ernest Hemingway, where the meaning simmers in the silence between words. Garcia/Hunter compositions are studies in paradox, minimalist tales of weak men raging mightily yet tragically against the night. The "old man down" in "Wharf Rat" is as vivid and specific as any character in American literature.

The lyrics of Robert Hunter can beam us into deep space where the dark star crashes and searchlights locate cracks in our denial, or into a backroom Reno betting parlor where the coffee is cold and all of the games are rigged, a condition that can only be trumped by voluntary craziness, wafting on a friendly wind that blows you safely home. Or take us on a visit with danger, up and close and personal with the desperadoes of "Jack Straw." How loaded with irony are the opening lines regarding sharing the women and the wine, for this is a song about what passes for trust in a world in which *no one knows how to share*. We visit the world of a dying man during his last minutes, through the voice of "Black Peter," and again there is a moment of enlightenment, that everything from birth on has led to this day, his last day, and yet there is nothing special about the day at all, it is a day like any other day, it just happens to be his last. Hunter's words can be a conduit into a sweaty world inhabited by the power-hungry lyricist himself, who yearns, hypothetically at least, for the ultimate power of the word—words that glow with the gold of sunshine when played on a stringless harp, words that tear loose from the axis and flicker with the shadows of flame. The hardscrabble, unvarnished, uncomplaining, and authentically American words to "Cumberland Blues" ("Lotta poor man got to walk the line / Just to pay his union dues") are so genuine that an actual miner complained that the Dead were making use of—stealing!—a local tune. Truth is, the lyrics are completely fictional, and derivative of nothing.

Love in Hunter's lyrics is something gone, never more heart-breakingly than in "Stella Blue" when he lays out the sad truth, ripping away the last gasp of denial, that everything from the sublime to the ridiculous, the poignant to the violent, the ecstatic to the tragic, the living to the dead, all rolls into one at the end, all stuff that comes with a cost, transient things, solid and within grasp one instant, gone forever the next.

Hunter came up with different textures for each era of the Dead's existence. He listened to his muses, tripped off to the far reaches of the solar system with his cat Susie, and after a while he realized that all lyrics didn't have to be "Dark Star," or "China Cat."

Hunter realized that he didn't need to explain the music of the spheres with each phrase. Sometimes it was sufficient merely to list the reasons why (first, Sweet Anne Marie; second, prison, baby) the hero cried away each lonely night.

There was a friendly, down-home appeal to the Dead, which allowed him an opportunity to be whimsical, although the only lyric he could recall that was 100 percent whimsy was "Ramble On Rose."

And he didn't need to sit and concentrate with a grunt and a furrowed brow on germinating the idea that might result in a song. All he had to do was leave his receivers on open and the ideas came.

Like that time when he was walking through Barcelona and he heard an incongruous sound, someone playing a Jew's harp. In Spain. How delightfully unlikely, and the next thing he knew he was singing to himself the words to what would become "Tennessee Jed."

These days Hunter is an old man who, after a spinal abscess but before the discovery of his Big C, was prescribed morphine for about a month, first time ever, and he realized how long it had been since he tried a new drug. Next thing you knew, he'd written lyrics for a couple of songs on Mickey's album.

Hunter, at seventy-two, cancer gone, decided to take his act on the road, even if he needed cheaters to remember his words. Eight dates, playing sixteen to eighteen songs a night, for the first time had peoples' phones shoved at him by the audience. With smart phones, everyone's a taper now.

You bet your ass he played Jerry songs, "the more bittersweet the better," Hunter says.

But maybe he snuck in a song or two he wrote with Dylan, the only guy he ever let change his words. The work with Dylan didn't make him feel all warm and fuzzy: after an initial get-together, much of it done on the phone, and via e-mail.

The pathways of communication between Hunter and the surviving members of the Dead remain cluttered with personal obstacles. When David Browne from *Rolling Stone* asked him how he liked those songs he'd written with Phil and Bobby for Further, Hunter said he didn't know, he'd never heard them. He remembered writing the words, and that was fun, but that was the last he'd heard about it. Had he ever been to a Further concert? No, but that was on him, he was lazy, never went to shows unless he was performing. Truth is, all the Dead myths got to him sometimes, the way kids looked at you and saw this legend all covered with the opaque patina of history, not seeing him as just a guy who likes to meet people and perform. He could grow distant if he didn't concentrate on engaging, getting into a deep conversation backstage with the first person who talks to him, and that cleanses off the phony vibe. He's written a novel and a half but hasn't much hope of publishing. He's been approached about a memoir but knew they'd want him to dissect his lyrics like lizard doctors encircling a cold steel operating table, and that was tedious. He'd rather his story in the Dead and with the Dead be told in the words to the songs. Besides, he's not a kiss-and-tell guy. A lot of what happened between him and the Dead stays between him and the Dead. As the boxing writer Bert Sugar once said to me, "Given a choice between myth and fact, go with myth every time." That said it all. Hunter didn't want his reality, his so-called details to chip away at the edges of a myth that makes millions of people happy. He was going out there with his acoustic guitar and he was going to deliver "Brokedown Palace"—and they were *supposed* to think of Jerry, and they were supposed to cry.

THE BAND HAS A PHILOSOPHY

The Grateful Dead philosophy eventually surpassed "it's cool to get high," and spread to matters of humanity, benevolence, charity, unity, and spirituality. One of the reasons that the band so drastically outlived the hippie/flower-power media car wreck is they never bought into the naïve optimism that turned its slogans into national catchphrases, that led to rose-colored notions that all you had to do was put a flower in the barrel of The Man's gun and there would be peace on Earth; that if you joined a commune in Big Sur then capitalism would melt like the wicked witch. The band knew better. You can't change everything forever. You can only change where you're at right now, and for a lot of people that's enough.

If an interviewer really pinned Jerry down, and it was hard to, because he would squirm—"Is there anything you *don't* like about drugs?"—he would say that it was the criminality. Make all drugs legal and the world would become better, not worse. Criminals would no longer be selling the shit. Consumers would know exactly what they were taking and how much they were taking. No more surprise trips to the john (or worse) because your coke has been cut with Ex-Lax. No more midnight ambulances to Bellevue because the China White was unexpectedly strong. Put real scientists to work making better drugs, drugs that are "good for you," he would say. Why are drugs illegal? Because the government doesn't want people changing their consciousness. Changed consciousness makes it easier to see through corporate and governmental bullshit. There is a glaze of propaganda covering everything in America, disseminated by the schools and the newspapers and the TV. Take drugs and that glaze peels away like latex under a blowtorch. Take drugs and you can *see*, see that taking drugs is no reason to throw people in jail. Sure, drugs were addictive, but the reason addicts got in trouble was because they committed crimes to buy drugs. Regulate the system and you'd have less of a drain on society, as addicts would need less medical care, and the number of functioning addicts would skyrocket. That last was supposed to sum up the argument, but just as often lost Jerry the day.

The band philosophy wasn't as much about what it took, as what it gave. The Dead formalized their charitable efforts and formed the Rex Foundation, named after Rex Jackson, the roadie and tour manager who was killed in a car accident in 1976. Each year, the Dead played a handful of shows with the band's portion of the proceeds going to fund a few handpicked causes. The board was made up of anonymous band members and board meetings sometimes got loud as they argued about who would and wouldn't get a check. The money did not all go to formal charities, but it did all go to nonprofit concerns, often projects or causes that weren't actively seeking money. The Dead took great delight in surprising people who were doing good works with big fat checks, just like the messenger on the old (1955–60) TV show, *The Millionaire*.*

A key portion of the Dead philosophy was to treat the Dead fan

---

*When one of their biggest—literally biggest—fans, seven-foot basketball star Bill Walton, told the Dead that the Lithuanian basketball team wasn't going to make it to the 1992 Summer Olympics for lack of bread, the band sold a T-shirt showing a skeleton slam-dunking a basketball (the author's all-time favorite, wore it till it fell apart), and sent the proceeds to Lithuania, where the hoopsters got to live their Olympic dream. That's the sort of thing that makes a band rich in a way no bank account can measure.

base right. (And this is a subject we'll look at more when discussing the Dead's innovative marketing techniques.) There would be no price gouging, and systems were designed so that the more dedicated a fan was, the better he or she was treated. The Dead had their own system for selling tickets by mail order so that fans didn't have to pay the enormous fees charged by other ticket services.

The only question worth asking was/is, "Are you kind?"

It didn't figure that this shy, chubby man would have the charisma, talent, and show-biz savvy to cast his spell over large masses of people. But there was nothing like the coiled-spring silence in a huge arena just before Jerry sang the words "Stella Blue." One example of Jerry's magic, one of thousands. Another: counterintuitively, he stepped up his game in the heat.

© Bob Minkin / www.minkinphotography.com

The Grateful Dead, not just a band that played songs, sold
records, and gave concerts, but a band of sorcerers, conjurers of
a rare and different tune, music with a heartbeat and breath.
© Bob Minkin / www.minkinphotography.com

The Grateful Dead sang songs that seemed to take
place in the Old West, where men's fates wriggled under the
thumb of circumstance. Bobby lived on a ranch, so that added
street cred. Tie-dye was discovered on Bobby's ranch!
© Bob Minkin / www.minkinphotography.com

The Dead as they appeared on November 24, 1978, still
carrying the flag (waving it wide and high) for freedom of spirit.
© Bob Minkin / www.minkinphotography.com

The Grateful Dead will
always matter because of the
genius music that offered so
many years of trippy pleasure,
especially Jerry's beam-me-up-
Scotty leads and achingly sad
vocals. Here Jerry is playing
the guitar he called Tiger.
© Bob Minkin / www
.minkinphotography.com

Jerry at Winterland in 1977 playing the guitar he called Wolf.
© Bob Minkin / www.minkinphotography.com

That moment of one-group mind when the music is
no longer being controlled by individuals, but by the group
itself, is one that Jerry called an "aural holograph."
© Bob Minkin / www.minkinphotography.com

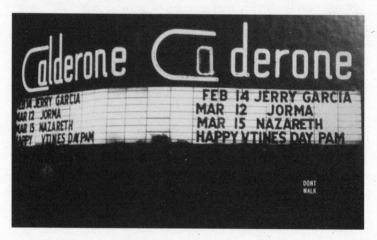

Nothing says, "I love you" like Valentine's Day and Jerry, especially
at the Calderone in Hempstead, New York. © Gregg Praetorius

The band changed when Phil joined. All of a sudden here's a guy
in the band who once wrote a symphony for four orchestras with the
audience in the middle, who discusses anti-notes, who says that in the
ultimate music there are no key signatures, no melodies, and who wants
to make improvisation and musical conversation a group focal point.
© Bob Minkin / www.minkinphotography.com

Ron "Pigpen" McKernan was an assemblage of contradictions,
a young white man who sounded like an old black man, a hippie who
was afraid of drugs but managed to drink himself to death at the age
of twenty-seven. He was also a brother to the rest of the band
and the number-one reason for the band's early success.
Art by Tekla Benson, TekBeDesign.com

OF ACADEMICS AND BUSINESS

Garcia and Hunter were wary of the corrupt power that big money might bring. When the Dead made the double live album known as *Live/Dead* in 1969, they wanted to give the record away. The record company talked them out of it, but did agree to sell it at a discount price, and it was the cheapest double album in the Warner Bros. Records catalog. The band knew, sort of, that they had to engage in business in order to survive as a self-sustaining entity, but they refused to buy into the standard band scheme: make and promote hit singles, milk every possible cent from their fans, and live in a mansion with a swimming pool. The Dead may have suffered because of their naïveté as capitalists, but they never buckled under and strayed from the path of fairness for all.

They thought like a nonprofit, for years putting most of their money into equipment and drugs.

• • •

In March 2010 the *Atlantic* magazine reported that "the Grateful Dead Archive" was to be opened to the public at the University of California at Santa Cruz. When the school first advertised for an archivist in 2009, Jon Stewart of TV's *The Daily Show* couldn't spit out the stoner jokes rapidly enough. The Dead turned over four decades of archival material to the school to be turned into an exhibit.

There were recordings and videos, the books that recorded expenses and earnings, press clippings, sets used for stage shows, letters to and from the band largely dealing with the band's fund-raising activities, a thank-you note from President Obama, some elaborately decorated fan letters.

The archives were of importance to several academic disciplines: sociology, philosophy, and ethnomusicology. It was because of that last specialty that the band chose UCSC for its archives. On its faculty was composer and ethnomusicologist Fredric Lieberman, who for years has been studying and teaching the Grateful Dead, offering a course that began as a more general one on American vernacular music. Teaching the Dead is no longer the rarity it once was, but Lieberman was by far the first. Back in the 1960s he'd studied under ethnomusicologist Charles Seeger, Pete's dad, and they agreed that popular and non-Western music were getting short shrift in the academic world. Lieberman was teaching classes of undergrads about acid tests and nightly journeys into "Space and Drums" in the early 1970s. In 1983, Mickey invited the prof to come along on tour and learn how everything worked, socially, musically, whatever. Sometimes you'll catch him in a film. He's the old guy, the scientist, crouching behind the rhythm section during a show, surreptitiously observing and scribbling notes into a book. The prof had the chance to see firsthand the ballbusting secret society that is the Grateful Dead, where the rules are you bust the balls of the guy who just busted your balls, and when in doubt bust Mickey's balls. The band has gone whole tours without playing certain songs simply because Mickey suggested they should.

The other top Dead authority in the academic world is the band's official archivist since 2010, Nicholas G. Meriwether, who studied history at Princeton and Cambridge, and archival practice at the University of South Carolina. In 2007, he published his Grateful Dead tome, an academic collection, *All Graceful Instruments: The Contexts of the Grateful Dead Phenomenon*, which assembles thirteen widely varying essays on the band into an "interdisciplinary anthology" about a "variegated cultural phenomenon," looking at the Dead through the lens of literary criticism, musicology, sociology, and philosophy. Meriwether was also was the band's bibliographer, expanding his list of relevant reading and listening into books called *Reading the Grateful Dead: A Critical Study*, and *Studying the Dead: The Grateful Dead Scholars Caucus, An Informal History*. The latter book tells the story of the Southwest/ Texas Popular Culture and American Culture Association's inauguration in 1998 of a separate section nicknamed the Grateful Dead Scholars Caucus. The caucus has produced more than three hundred scholarly articles in the years of its existence, which have resulted in more than one hundred publications and a dozen books.

Meriwether told the website ilovelibraries.org that the notion of a Dead archives was first bounced around as early as the 1970s, when it was considered a subcategory to in-house records management and publicity. For years the archive was kept by the Dead's Eileen Law.

There had been much made about the archive's unique nature. Grateful Dead. Archive. What a juxtaposition! But Meriwether never saw it as weird. Indeed, it seemed like a natural progression from other collections the school had taken on, including those of Beat poets Lawrence Ferlinghetti and Kenneth Patchen, and composer Lou Harrison. As band archivist, Meriwether's duties included editing and publishing material on the Grateful Dead ranging from a newsletter to a peer-reviewed scholarly journal. He was also in charge of, as he listed it, "acquisitions, donations, development, outreach, and public service."

Some people are disappointed by how much the Dead archive is the same as other scholarly collections. It works the same. You register and peruse material in the reading room. There are always new items being made available to readers. The obsessed may visit frequently and still not run out of new things to read. Then there is the 1,400-square-foot exhibit space that features rotating themes and exhibits. You know you're onto something that people find fascinating and valuable when you start running into counterfeits, such as a recent ticket that purported to be to the Dead's first electric gig ever at Magoo's Pizza in Menlo Park but turned out to be a hoax.

Meriwether loves the job. Sometimes it's like being in show business, sometimes like working in charity work or in a museum, and, when it was most fun, like being a detective, trying to identify the artists for early Dead posters. Sometimes it's Moby Grape's drummer's cousin-in-law, or something, and that's a fun investigation. Meriwether has met all surviving Dead musicians, and has had several meetings with musicians regarding the archives. But usually he communicates with band members, if necessary, through a liaison like official legacy manager and vault archivist David Lemieux (of *Dave's Picks* fame). It wouldn't be a Dead thing if it wasn't cyber-hip, and the archives have their own Facebook page, useful in tracking down a donor or to ID an artist, but mostly to stay in touch with the people who cared the most, the Dead marketing strategy since they first learned what marketing meant. Meriwether says there won't be an archives for very long if no one comes to see it. Staying popular is key, he says, "The archive doesn't just record the band, it records the entire phenomenon, which can be thought of as every step in a chain of communication from the moment of artistic creation to its broader reception in the audience and beyond." (Want to know more? Visit www.gdao.org.)

But none of this was the angle that attracted *Atlantic* magazine to the story. Nope, they were excited about what the archive might have to teach us about *business*. The Dead weren't always the best judges of character when it came to trusting people with the money, but in the long run the machine ran without any polluting exhaust or depletion. For all of that hippie disorganization, the Dead were "visionary geniuses" when it came to creating "customer value," promoting social networking, and formulating innovative business strategy. Some of those innovations are:

1 Sell your best tickets to your best fans. Being loyal to the Dead meant they would be loyal to you. Attend every concert and chances were good you'd be the first to learn of upcoming concert dates, be afforded discount prices by buying directly from the band, and soon be in the front row.
2 Transform clients into advocates. By rewarding loyalty with an inside status (first through a mailing list, then through the Internet), fans became evangelical, singing the praises of the Dead and recruiting new members to the fold.
3 Encourage rather than ban bootlegging. By partnering with tapers rather than shutting them down, and signing licensing deals that allowed fans to use Dead logos on their products, the pirates became a referral service, sharing with nonfans and further enlarging the flock.

Here in Northern California in the hallowed halls of a university library, we get a strong sense of why the Grateful Dead matter. Here is academic affirmation of something Owsley and the tapers had believed for decades, the Dead deserve a complete record because everything they ever did together or in parts was worth remembering. It *all matters*.

Before the archive opened it was under such tight security that you might've thought the vault contained a sarcophagus from a cursed Egyptian tomb. There was concern that, among the Dead zealots, there might be one who either wanted to steal things or harm the archives because, like the name of the band, the concept was too intense. For East Coast fans, a separate archive exhibit could be seen in the not-as-stuffy-as-it-used-to-be New-York Historical Society, whose steadfast refusal to lose its anachronistic hyphen was once-but-no-more indicative of a staid temperament. There one could see a copy of the Winter 1972 issue of the *Journal of Psychedelic Drugs*, a periodical for medical pros that also sold well in head shops alongside the incense, pipe screens, and black-light posters, and in it is the first mention of the Dead in a medical journal, a study of emergency treatment records at a variety of rock shows which demonstrated conclusively that Dead fans tended toward blotter bummers while Led Zeppelin fans were prone to alcohol poisoning.

Back to business, the Dead invented practices—focusing intensely on their most loyal fans, creating and delivering superior loyal-customer service—that have been adopted by corporate America. The Dead incorporated early, established a board of directors consisting of members of the band, crew, and front office. Their merchandising always felt like it was handled with love, and the fans never felt exploited. Taping was allowed, under the correct assumption that tape sharing would widen the fan base. While the world has largely caught up, they were innovators at cyber-marketing.

As is true of hookers, age brings respectability to rock stars. Gettysburg College philosophy professor Steve Gimbel wrote a book called *The Grateful Dead and Philosophy*, in which he wrote, "Revolutionaries get vilified, and then, once they get older, they just become cute. Think of Oscar Wilde. Once they're not dangerous anymore, it's okay to discuss them in serious ways." John Lennon and Muhammad Ali also come to mind.

For those interested in more about the Dead's innovative business practices, check out *Radical Marketing: From Harvard to Harley, Lessons from Ten That Broke the Rules and Made It Big*, by *New*

York Times reporter Glenn Rifkin, which has a whole chapter dedicated to the Grateful Dead.*

. . .

The Thirty-fifth Annual Southwest Popular/American Culture Association Conference (also known as the Seventeenth Annual Grateful Dead Scholars Caucus) was held in February 2014 at the Hyatt Regency in Albuquerque, New Mexico, and was heavily covered, in all of its "myriad aspects," by gratefuldead.net. With lectures and discussions led by fifty Grateful Dead scholars, the conference drew more than a thousand academics. For many it was Old Home Week, rekindling old friendships from previous caucuses. Topics of discussion: Deadhead identity; musicological investigation of "Dark Star"; and guest appearances by Grateful Dead family members turned authors Rosie McGee and Rhoney Stanley. Philosophers had their say. The accountants talked about how the Dead revolutionized marketing.

But that was during the day. After dinner the lights were dimmed and there was music, a concert by Dead biographer David Gans, plus a hootenanny. The itinerary was full. If you wanted to, and many did, you could go from first thing in the morning to past midnight and never have to eat, drink, hear, or speak anything except Dead. "We think all day and rock all night," is a common slogan.

Although the event has grown clubby over the years with so

---

*That marketing strategy continues today. If you haven't already, visit the website www.dead.net, and subscribe to their monthly bulletin, which shows up in your morning e-mail like a cup of strong coffee. You can order one or a thousand taped concerts, listen to back editions of *The Grateful Dead Hour*, read interviews, follow news, get tour info, or look at "Comix" (illustrated song lyrics) by Tim Truman. Plus, come the holidays, there's one-stop shopping for Christmas hippies and Hannukah heads alike.

many repeaters, it is very much *of* the Dead and that means inclusion rather than exclusion. The caucus tries to present a varied program. Over the years the attendees have been addressed by more than 150 scholars from twenty-six different fields and disciplines, ranging in experience and ability from senior professors to interested outsiders who just wander in. Bottom line, if you have an interesting topic, everyone will want to hear you out. If you are vapid or simply pushing a tangential agenda, folks might not be quite so patient. The rule is, if you want to be invited back, you will work hard on your presentation. People pay to attend, and the intention is to give everyone their money's worth.

OF MOUNTAIN GIRL

Long before she'd ever heard of the Warlocks, Carolyn Adams was on the cutting edge of psychedelic culture, riding with the Merry Pranksters to Millbrook and back. She was born and raised in Poughkeepsie, New York, was kicked out of high school, traveled west with her brother, and met Neal Cassady, who introduced her to Ken Kesey, who put her on the bus. When she got back west, to Haight-Ashbury, she saw and heard Jerry play his guitar and got it right away. This was greatness, Jerry as a person, as an icon, as a musician, the music itself, greatness. Folks that were there remember her standing right in front of the stage, looking just like R. Crumb drew her, beaming up at Jerry, already scheming ways to help support the greatness, to help it *grow*. She would offer her body to him, of course, but she would also facilitate his life. She'd clean up and cook and do laundry, stuff that Jerry wouldn't do if she weren't there, and keep him as healthy as possible. He was a fixer-upper, to put it mildly, living on cigarettes and Twinkies, never even finding the urge to empty the ashtray, which was heaping with butts and overflowing onto the floor. Mountain Girl, one of Kesey's friends called her that and the name stuck, was the first of the clan to figure out there were cool and uncool drugs. If there was a certain look in someone's eyes she'd grab him by the shirt, throw him against the wall, and roll up his sleeves to check for needle marks. When Mountain Girl first entered Jerry's life at the acid test in the Fillmore Auditorium, there were sparks. (As an East

Coast kid I'd always thought that the Fillmore Auditorium and the Fillmore West were the same arena, the name change being necessitated by the opening of the Fillmore East in New York. But no. When Bill Graham gave up control of the building known as the Fillmore Auditorium, he moved his operation into the former Carousel—a plush 1930s ballroom, chandeliers, red velour ceiling, owned by the League of Irish Voters—and changed its name to the Fillmore West.) In the house on Ashbury Jerry and Mountain Girl would disappear into Jerry's room and no one would see them for *days*. She never had a defined role in the band. They tried putting her on the soundboard for a brief time but she had little ones —one of Kesey's, two of Jerry's—to take care of and forgot when to pot up and down on the mikes. That was all right. She'd accomplished her goal. By the time she and Jerry split, he had a whole crew to empty his ashtrays and make sure he ate real food now and again.

Gregg Praetorius remembered that, of the many musical acts he'd worked with, Jerry was the only one who brought along his own stove and cook. That was about 1981, and the cook's name was Cy Kosis, and he was a culinary arts legend. According to veterans of the road, the one thing that wears down travelers more quickly than anything else is bad food. Cy Kosis saw to it that Jerry ate healthy food every day, and it's not unimportant to note that the years he cooked for Jerry were also those when Jerry appeared to be in the best shape with his weight under control. Working alongside Cy Kosis for a spell was Phil Guiliano, who expanded the idea and provided food-catering services for large tours such as those of Paul McCartney, Madonna, Eric Clapton, and the Rolling Stones.

Phil's dad called MG "Mountain Dew," which she dug—but *only* when Mr. Lesh was saying it. In the midseventies, she published a book about growing pot outdoors called *Primo Plant*, still available on Amazon.com. Today she remains on the board of the Rex Foundation, the Further Foundation, the Marijuana Policy Project, and is a former board member of the Women's Visionary Council. Long after they stopped being a romantic item, a lifetime later it seemed, Jerry and Mountain Girl were married in Oakland. It was in 1981, six years after they'd broken up, wed for tax purposes, but it never seems inappropriate when she's listed as one of Jerry's wives. When he needed it most, she was Jerry's ol' lady.

DEADHEADS ROAM THE EARTH

While Dead fans are a cross section of society, nomadic Deadheads skew demographically to the young, white, and carefree—the sort of people who can get away with running away with a band. To an outsider they can all seem exactly the same.

Rebecca G. Adams was a sociologist at the University of North Carolina in Greensboro, and in the late 1980s studied Deadheads as a sociological phenomenon. Professor Adams came into her study with the thought that the Deadheads formed what she called a "lifestyle enclave," a way of avoiding life rather than living it, and couldn't form meaningful relationships, but discovered the opposite to be true. She took classes on field trips to circulate among the tribe and to experience a Dead show, and she wrote about the Deadheads in a manner that treated them as a cutting-edge contemporary community, in such a way that she instantly became famous. All was going well until a conservative politician blasted the state of higher education, and used Adams's study of Deadheads to illustrate the decline, and she was forced to move on to subjects that reflected better on her school. But it was too late. The Deadheads were out there, now like the band itself clearly *worthy of academic study*. The academics didn't stop coming around just because of some Republican blasting.

The Grateful Dead cultivated a community focused on happiness, cut from a different cloth than other groups' fans. Deadheads didn't wait patiently for the band to come to an arena near them. Impenitent, they gathered into a pastoral tribe, like the Negritos of Southeast Asia and the San of Africa, and hit the road with the band.

Grateful Dead lyricist John Barlow said in 1982 that modern communities were no longer based on geography or necessity. The Deadheads formed a community that transcended locality, but remained tight nonetheless, as tight as any mining town in the USA. Barlow wasn't sure if this was a symptom of the downfall of locality-based communities, but it certainly could have been. People didn't come from anywhere anymore. The suburbs were rootless, so impersonal that people could live their entire lives in one spot, move, and not have a single neighbor they yearned to go back and visit. People were connected in new ways, and apt to feel closest to people with whom they shared a passion—soap operas, mystery novels, or Grateful Dead music. Social media has now formalized this pattern.

· · ·

Deadhead Nation is a phenomenon that has been imitated since by fans of other bands like Phish, but the nomadic Deadheads set a social precedent, neo-gypsies camping out in parking lots and public parks, selling paraphernalia and souvenirs to the locals to stay fed. The parking lot outside a Dead show was called "Shakedown Street," and from there the vendors hawked food and drink, T-shirts, stickers, and posters while generally putting off the rest of their lives in dedication to the Grateful Dead.

As the band aged, and their fans at home listening to the stereo aged, the touring Deadheads stayed the same age. For every oldster who got off the ride, a youngster climbed on, until a full generation separated the following pack and the band. Old farts like Phil and Hunter were being asked questions they couldn't have conceived of while riding the undulations in the walls of the Avalon Ballroom.

"Do you feel *parental* toward your young nomad fans?" reporters asked.

All who were asked were horrified at the notion. If kids were looking to the Dead to tell them who to be and what to do, they were wasting their time. The band said be whoever you want to be, do whatever you want to do. They were anti-parental. Forget what you hear, forget words of "wisdom," get outside and have a look all around for your *own self*.

· · ·

What was the biggest difference between the Dead and their fans? Satisfaction. The Deadheads saw themselves as blessed escapees from the Island of Misfit Toys, and were perfectly happy with whatever the band gave them. The band, on the other hand, couldn't think that way. The days of the acid tests were long gone. They had ambition in the sense that they wanted to be better than they were. Every show, to some extent, was a disappointment to a group of musicians who did not think in terms of how good it was, but of how good it could have been. The freaks in the crowd never had any sense of that. The band was always pleased that the Deadheads were there and that they were clearly having a good time, but the musicians were often alone in the room-for-improvement tent.

The musicians, Jerry in particular, became aware of the divine aura in which they were seen, but they didn't buy into it. You only had to look at the bad end that awaited most cult leaders to see what a trap that was. It was cool that there were dialed-in freaks out there in the dark who reported a group-mind experience, and sometimes a direct telepathic connection to what was happening on stage. If it was real, the musicians weren't feeling it. They had no sense of being puppet masters pulling their audience's strings. They were simply filling the air with wonderful sound, and everyone was free to get off on that in any way they chose.

A reporter once asked Jerry if the Dead could control the weather. He said no. As horseman Ed Behringer once said, "You can't control the weather, but you can control the atmosphere." That was the deal. The notes changed. The town changed. The vibe stayed the same.

Jerry said that his consciousness came in levels during the course of a show. First, he related to his guitar, then to the other members of the band, and third and last, to the members of the audience. On the occasions when he got to the third level, where his conscious mind was so in tune with what he was playing and how it related to what everyone else was playing, so that he could think about the audience, it wasn't necessarily a good thing. The music might have been perfect but perfect music was often snoozeville. The shows the audiences liked the most were the ones where Jerry could barely get to the first level of consciousness, where there was a struggle between himself and his guitar, and when he got it right, which was only some of the time, the audience lit up because they could feel the effort that went into it.

One of the ways Jerry avoided the "ego trap" was to believe that the music was not something he created but rather something he channeled, that it was in the air and that he and the Dead, if they had their heads right, would make it audible, and the difference between a great show and a lousy one was their ability to snatch the music out of the ozone and blast it out their speakers. If the show was awesome, man, Jerry couldn't take credit. Fame was an illusion. He was merely the conduit for the life energy, dig? If someone asked him what the hell that meant, he'd shrug (and think silently, *it don't mean shee-it*) and say that defining it was someone else's job. Sure, he was aware that people had weird imaginary things happen to them while listening to the Dead, that they passed out, had vivid religious experiences (Jerry on a cross with a crown of roses, aarrgghh!), were beamed up by flying saucers, but he tried hard not to think about it. The instant he thought, gee, if I play this song this way someone might have a religious experience, then he was a *fascist*.

At some point the band and its fans merged into an ever-growing and spiritual family. Some of them had a touch of gray now, but they were still out there, leaping with joy like children at shows by Further, Bembe Orisha, the Other Ones, Phil & Friends, Billy and the Trichromes, the Rhythm Devils, and RatDog. They kept the song lit.

And while memories of these bands live on, the weight of time is forcing them off the road. In April 2013, during a Further concert at the Capitol Theatre in Port Chester, New York, Bobby fell on stage while playing "Unbroken Chain." A crew member brought out a chair and he finished the song sitting. When the song was finished he was helped off stage and did not return. A statement released after that show said he would be "unable to perform in any capacity for the next several weeks." Fans, of course, were brittle with apprehension, and Bobby had nothing but reassurance for them. No, he wasn't going to be on stage any time soon, but that didn't mean he wasn't busy, making a record of original cowboy songs with Josh Ritter and the Yellowbirds' Josh Kaufman, transforming Dead songs into a symphony charted for an orchestra, "sort of producing" an opera. No worries. Then Bobby announced in August 2014 that RatDog's upcoming concert dates were being canceled. No reason was given, but it was largely assumed that health had a lot to do with it. Concert promoter John Scher told *Rolling Stone*, "Bobby's been having health problems for a while and now there are plenty of people who support him and want to help him get the care he needs."

In November 2014, Phil and Bobby announced there would be no more Further, their touring side project since 2009. They announced on the Further website, "We'll all be keeping very busy over the foreseeable future, and it's time to let Further take a bow. We enjoyed the ride more than we can possibly express." Further grew out of a brief tour by The [no Grateful] Dead, a band that featured the omnipresent Warren Haynes (Allman Brothers Band, Gov't Mule) as lead guitarist. The Dead shows were in support of Barack Obama's first presidential campaign. Further had not played since January 2014, when they performed four shows at the Paradise Waits Festival in Mexico. Not that there were any Mexicans in the crowd, a fact that frustrated Bobby. "It would be nice to see our Americana songbook resonate elsewhere in the world," he said, conceding that a good deal of public-relations work would be necessary first.

The November announcement fueled belief that a Dead reunion might be in the works to commemorate the Grateful Dead's fiftieth anniversary. Pouring gasoline on that fire were Bobby's comments to *Rolling Stone*, that "We have to do something commemorative. I think we owe it to the fans, we owe it to the songs, we owe it to ourselves. If there are issues we have to get past, I think we owe it to ourselves to man up and get past them. If there are hatchets to be buried, then let's get to work. Let's start digging. I'll just say, to my delicate sensibilities, that it would be wrong to let [the anniversary] go by un-commemorated." Of course, if pinned down, he'd have to admit that, as far as he was concerned, the fiftieth anniversary had already come and gone, that nothing magic happened when the band changed their name, and he counted his experiences with the Warlocks as all part of the same trip. A half-century is a long time, but it hasn't blunted Bobby's need to improvise on stage. Speaking in his unique vernacular, he said, "After you've played a song a few hundred times, little surprises mean a lot. And you only get those surprises if you hold the skunk. And so, we've got to stretch them out, we've got to see what else the song has to reveal. . . . Songs are living things. It's a different life form, but they grow. Some songs go to sleep for a while. 'Dark Star' went to sleep for a long time and then came back."

While Lesh and Weir were announcing the end of a side project, Bill Kreutzmann was announcing the beginning of a new one. During the summer of 2014, he told Benjy Eisen of *Rolling Stone* that he was "convening" a new band to be called The Locknstep Allstars, featuring bassist Oteil Burbridge from the Allman Brothers Band, keyboardist Aron Magner of the Disco Biscuits, and guitarist Steve Kimock from RatDog. Solid, but the most exciting news was that they'd be playing with a series of guest stars, most notably Taj Mahal, who first sat in with the Dead in 1968. Bill said he got the idea while "revisiting" the Dead's career and their attempt to make every performance different. He was taking it to the next step. With every performance the performers themselves would be different, a shuffling lineup, heading into new territory. That was the most important aspect, as far as Bill was concerned. He had no interest in recreating anything, or to compete with previous achievements. "Nobody's going to fill in for Jerry Garcia. We tried that. It's impossible."

• • •

Before we say goodbye to Deadhead Nation, let's take a look at one female Deadhead, a spinner, who in 2015 is getting to an age —pushing thirty—where spinning is becoming increasingly difficult. It is a young woman's game to spin, and she, although she still appears young and beautiful, is a veteran of the road. She tells me that she thinks musicians are magicians, she doesn't understand how to make music so it really does seem magical, and that she is sublimating her life with the alchemy of their song. She understands that the band, whatever 2015 jam band with Dead credibility it happens to be, is trying to meld minds inside the music so that the music becomes a greater consciousness like hive intelligence in comparison to a single bee. The spinners, she says, are basically trying to do the same thing, but using a different medium. The flow you had to get into in order to lose yourself in the dance was the same flow the musicians tap into trying to lose themselves in the song.

These days she's taking it easy and bumming about life. Back pain has become constant, maybe slight scoliosis. She recently went to see John (Dark Star Orchestra, Further) Kadlecik's new band, the Golden Gate Wingmen, and was able to dance and have a lot of fun, but afterwards she spent a couple of days in bed feeling like she'd been hit by a truck. She's hoping this isn't a permanent thing, that she'll still be able to twirl to the fullest extent.

"I'll be OK as long as I can dance!" she says.

21

CRICKETS PLAYED
ON *BLUES FOR ALLAH*

And it had nothing to do with Buddy Holly's famous back-up band.

Blues for Allah was the Dead's eighth studio record, released during the late summer of 1975, after being recorded that spring. It's the record with the fiddle-playing high-priest skeleton on the cover. In addition to his red robe, he's wearing wraparound shades. It meant the first appearance of Mickey Hart on a Dead record since he left the band soon after the completion of *Workingman's Dead*, almost five years earlier. The record's FM hit was "Franklin's Tower," which blasted out of many a dorm window during the first weeks of my sophomore year at Hofstra. Everyone was rolling away the dew. Which dew? Dog do? Probably the morning dew, couldn't be sure.

There were elements of *Blues for Allah* that were missed on the music when blasted over the quad by dinosaur-sized speakers. Quieter listeners in ridiculously large headphones knew something was going on, but perhaps not what. What were those strange sounds on side two? Was it Jerry's guitar processed and synthesized through a new gizmo? Nope.

According to Mickey Hart, the band acquired and miked a box of rare and wonderful crickets. They made a series of short cricket recordings, sped some up, slowed some down, played some forward and some backward, so that some sounded like whales while others sounded like birds, and distributed the crickets across side two of the record. A voltage-controlled amplifier was used to make it sound as if the desert itself were whispering "Allah." A lot of neat stuff, no doubt cost-foolish, and perhaps one of the reasons it was decided to go with record producers who demanded professional decision-making when knocking out potential hit songs for their next few subpar studio LPs.

What happened to the crickets? When the band was done with them, they were granted their freedom on Bobby's mountain. For years Bobby had exotic crickets playing music outside his bed-room window.

The crickets magically reappeared at a party in San Francisco's Great American Music Hall, where Mickey decided to use a box of them during the playing of "Unusual Occurrences." A sand-filled box of the little fellers was placed near a microphone. Trouble was, as the song went on, the crickets escaped from the box, and the call went out, "More crickets!" So the sound guy had to repeatedly pot up on that mike to compensate.

22

DEAD WORLD IS A
KINDER, GENTLER PLACE

The sixties were a domestically combative time, freaks versus pigs
(that is, police), adults versus kids, straight versus stoned, war versus antiwar. Given this fact, it is amazing that the Dead often had
the wisdom to see through the stereotypes.

Let's start by saying that the Dead had seen enough bad polic-
ing to turn on all cops at all times. Once the Dead played a show
in Boston and four thousand more people showed up than there
were tickets. When the people didn't leave fast enough the cops
maced them. It was enough to make them wonder about what
they did for a living. What was the point of putting on a show
when you were just leading kids into a trap?

So you'd think that they'd be on the kids' side all the time, right?
Nope, the Dead called them the way they saw them.

When the Dead were part of the traveling Festival Express that
crossed Canada by train in 1970, they encountered "hippies" that,
having heard that Woodstock turned into a "free concert, man,"
figured they didn't have to buy a ticket. All they needed to do was
show up and they'd be let into the show. Told this made no eco-
nomic sense, they became rowdy, eh. In one city the Dead were
forced to play a (very short) free concert just to avoid trouble.
Throughout the day the RCMP was the voice of reason. Bobby told
a reporter, "The cops have been cool. It's the kids that are assholes."

Naturally, that is the exception to the rule, and the Dead were always a persuasive voice against the "evil" aspects of straight culture: Wall Street, the military-industrial complex, intolerance, and yes, Gestapo-like law enforcement. Their liberal voice remained clear and strong even as the country shifted to the right during the Reagan/Bush era. The facets of straight culture that were not perceived as evil (such as religion and domesticity) largely received a pass from the band. Jerry, with a Spanish dad and an Irish mom, was raised very Catholic, went to church until he was ten or eleven and was never confirmed, said he thought real Christianity was OK, not perfect. It was kind of weird when it came to death, taking what is clearly an abstract concept, what happens to consciousness when the body ceases to live, and overly personifying it into a concept (heaven) that the masses could get a grip on. Regarding post-death consciousness, Jerry doesn't want to use his cigarette to bust anyone's helium balloon, so he says why would the universe bother to have consciousness evolve if it just ended with death. Regarding Catholicism, he didn't care for the exclusivity clause, but a lot of the rules for behavior set forth, the commandments, are the bedrock of civilized behavior. What religion really needed to make it a solid positive was ritual celebration, more singing and less listening, being preached to—but maybe no. If churches were better at ritual celebration, fewer people would come to Grateful Dead shows. People accept Dead shows as an almost religious experience because it has ritual celebration, a ritual performed in a trustworthy environment. Fans feel comfortable in a predictable vibe, taking it closer to the edge at a Dead show than say, a show by the Who. If pressed Jerry would admit he had no clue if there was a God, but religion taught some important lessons. Don't fall into the ego trap. Respect others. That stuff he could dig. Once Jerry felt he was having a conversation with a higher intelligence, very cool, might've been God, the idea was exciting. Then he noticed that God had exactly the same sense of humor that he did.

Whenever Phil catches Jerry talking theology, he has the same interjection, "God isn't dead, he's just a beautiful joke." Mr. Natural was down with that.

Now maybe having the Dead as your religion is helpful to you, a golden road along your pursuit of happiness, that's cool, but what if—David Gans asked Jerry—the Dead is a harmful drug to some people, causing souls to act like moths to the flame? What if obsessively listening to the Dead sucks them into a world that is harmful to them? Jerry said he tries to concentrate on the joy he's giving people, and he thinks of the Dead in those terms. He is psychologically savvy to know that obsessives might grow attached to the music and the scene, but if it weren't for the Dead it would be UFOs or comic-book collecting to the point of hoarding, or whatever, something else to obsess over. They weren't causing the obsessiveness; they were merely the ones being obsessed over. Jerry would have liked to think the Dead were better for a troubled mind than watching the skies for an alien invasion, or living among ceiling-high stacks of Gilbert Shelton's *The Fabulous Furry Freak Brothers* and *Fat Freddy's Cat*, but maybe not.

• • •

Longtime Dead promoter John Scher feels the Dead's influence today goes beyond the music: "Other than the Beatles, they are the most important sociological force in music history." Scher notes that they lived by their creed—live free, be happy—and put their audience first. They kept their tickets reasonably priced. They steadfastly set examples of how society should live: treat each other kindly; a friend of yours is a friend of mine. There are still millions of Deadheads all over the world, everywhere from San Francisco to Berlin, when Scher travels he is apt to see a Deadhead in a Grateful Dead hat or a tie-dyed shirt. And these people in the hats and the shirts are sixty years old, they've lived their lives following the

Grateful Dead's sociological map, so in that way the band made the world a less selfish, and more mellow and caring place.

Scher says that in terms of the music mattering, the Dead were thought of as a sixties band but were far more relevant in the 1970s. The thing that differentiated them from the other bands of their ilk, like the Airplane, was that, without shifting to being a pop band, they wrote more great songs than almost any other group from the 1960s until now, except the Beatles.

"Between all of their writers, the Dead recorded about twenty-five great songs, with a good beat, and easy to dance to, to use the old Dick Clark line," Scher says. And they did it without actually having a hit single.

Scher feels there were eight to ten songs from *Workingman's Dead* and *American Beauty* that, produced differently, could have been the Eagles. When the Dead did finally have a hit and "Touch of Grey" went to number 9 on *Billboard*'s Hot 100 singles chart on August 15, 1987, it was sort of a mistake, and ended up doing them more harm than good. Their following, which was already very big, became so huge that it was unmanageable.

Scher was promoting all of their shows at that time, except for the ones on the West Coast. His company spent three-quarters of its time dealing with questions of security and medical facilities. They would send the venues well in advance a twenty-page booklet that let everyone know what was in store for them, that it didn't make any difference what they did, they were going to have a certain number of people camping out in the parking lot, a certain number of people were going to need medical attention, so they should be prepared, so there were never any surprises.

• • •

Dead photographer and sometime lecturer Jay Blakesberg says that the Dead completely changed his life.

"They changed me as a human being in general, but especially as a creative human being," he says.

Blakesberg feels honored to be part of that zeitgeist, of the select few who, over the course of thirty-five years, had his life enriched by the band's music, lyrics, and life-affirming adventure.

Deadhead Jay Bianchi says: "The band is an ongoing link to the most pivotal time in American history in terms of social changes. They represent the freedom that is America, they are not just an American band, but what it means to be American in a good way."

Their music personified freedom and innocence, and their tours provided the counterculture with a destination to run away to, a circus of sorts where all your friends would be.

"The great society was built as a moving circus with no rules except common sense and love," Bianchi says. "As you experience each and every song it opens up a whole new world that allows you to travel and transcend time. It is through the Grateful Dead that I have understood my parents, become friends with my brothers, and became who I am."

To sum it all up, though, we turn again to Augustus Owsley "Bear" Stanley III, who said, "The Dead are magic personified."*

---

*Owsley passed away, moved on to another plane of consciousness, on March 12, 2011, having survived throat cancer only to die in a car accident.

23

THEIR MOST SPONTANEOUS
MOMENT BECAME THEIR
FINEST HOUR

During the first months of 1968 the sun never shone on a Sunday in
San Francisco, a lousy city to live in if you enjoy baking in the sun
—sophisticated as all get-out but foggy. Then there came a Sunday when the sky was cloudless and blue, so every ambulatory soul
was outside walking around, enjoying the day, which in some sections of the city can cause a concentrated mixture of pedestrians
and motor traffic. In the Haight a car hit a pedestrian, the police
came in like gangbusters, and managed to trigger a riot that resulted in a scary influx of military gear and seventy-five disheveled
freaks spending the night in the hoosegow. Relations between the
freak community and the police were chillier than the Tenderloin
at dawn until the city sought to make amends for what they now
tacitly acknowledged as a colossal overreaction. They announced
that all of Haight Street would be closed to traffic and would be
a pedestrian mall on Sunday, March 3, 1968. When the day came,
the Dead simply showed up and played. They never asked anyone's permission about anything, and worked on the assumption
that there was no one in charge. All of the band rode the truck
with the equipment except Jerry who approached unmolested on
foot with his guitar in his hand. They showed up, announced that
they were the band, and started to set up. To get electricity they
ran an extension cord through a window in the Straight Theatre.

You've probably seen the photo. The Dead on their flatbed truck while in the distance narrow Haight Street is packed with people as far as the eye can see, people are watching from the windows of buildings on both sides. Phil says that was the best it got, that day, yet another sunny Sunday, with the Grateful Dead smoothing out "the whole world of confrontation and conflict."

THEY OVERCAME SO MUCH
AND FORGED ON

A lesser, mere mortal band would have been torn asunder by the things the Dead shrugged off. Here's a partial list:

- Pigpen got too sick to play and died.
- Their first effort on their own record label, grateful Dead Records, was the studio LP *Wake of the Flood*, which was bootlegged and distributed by pirates, skimming sales away from the neo-businessmen.
- Mickey's dad was the manager for a while, talking himself into the role by playing a Bible-thumper who was going to do the Lord's work by protecting these righteous hippies from the big bad corporate pigs. They were deeply in debt by the time they realized that Lenny Hart had a very weird way of keeping the books and was burning them like a city-park dealer with bags of oregano. Shit kept happening. Pigpen got a new keyboard and it was pulled off the stage by a repo man. Jerry's check for his work on the soundtrack for the artsy film *Zabriskie Point* disappeared. Then Lenny split to Mexico, vanished, with a new girlfriend, a bank employee who helped him vamoose with—according to Dennis McNally, the band's official historian—$155,000 from the Dead's bank vault. According to the song "He's Gone," Lenny Hart would "steal your face right off your head." There was no indication that Mickey knew anything about it or was

responsible for the financial irresponsibility—or, for that matter, that the Dead held a grudge against Mickey because of what Lenny had done. But it ate at Mickey anyway. Despondent, Mickey quit in shame.

- Keith Godchaux went into a dark place and his wife Donna Jean went pitchy. They had troubles with each other, marital in nature, and once made like demolition derby, each in their own car, in a mostly empty studio parking lot.

- Jerry became reliant on cocaine and heroin, packed on the poundage, and developed hygiene issues. The hard stuff began to affect Jerry's performances in 1984, when during the East Coast swing of a tour, he took the stage listless and not fully engaged. When the tour was over he went into his apartment and didn't come out. The band attempted several interventions, but nothing stuck for long, and Jerry's health continued heading south until he slipped into a diabetic coma—dreamed he was in a futuristic spaceship with giant insects, came out of it and felt himself comprised of protoplasm chunks held together by weak perforated links like stamps, vegetables spoke to him in comically ethnic accents, and there were tiny cockroach-like things crawling through his bloodstream, lasted for a couple of days—and when he snapped out of it, Mountain Girl and Robert Hunter were at his bedside sitting vigil, and his synapses were scrambled so badly that, while he was still wondering if it were true that there were bugs inside your body and you could speak with immigrant vegetables, he had to relearn how to play guitar.

- Keith (at age thirty-two in a car accident) and Brent Mydland (of a speedball OD, last binge before a planned rehab, at age thirty-seven) became the second and third Dead keyboardists to die. In 2006 Brent's replacement, Vince Welnick, formerly of the Tubes and Todd Rundgren, committed suicide and became the fourth—and still there were applicants to fill the job. Amazingly, Tom Constanten and Bruce Hornsby both tickled the ivories for the former Warlocks and lived.

- The band made a series of studio albums for Arista Records that pretty much sucked because, as Mickey Hart put it, they were produced by "twits and plumbers." (Keith Olsen, *Terrapin Station*, 1977; Lowell George of Little Feat, *Shakedown Street*, 1978; Gary Lyons, producer for Aerosmith and Foreigner, *Go to Heaven*, 1979—all with "different levels of consciousness about it.") People might not like the results all of the time but each of those producers took the time to learn what the Dead were all about before trying to pigeonhole the group into a commercially viable comfort zone like disco or adult-oriented rock. It is perhaps revealing that Bobby sang the praises of these producers before and after working with them, and asked Gary Lyons to produce a record for Bobby and the Midnites. Jerry found polite things to say about the producers; he was pleased that they all asked questions that made musical sense and when addressed to him, he was pleased they were questions to which he usually knew the answer. Jerry said it was interesting to hear what other people could do with the Dead if given the opportunity. Although *Terrapin Station* had some punch, and a centerpiece that was musically more complex than anything the Dead had done before, *Shakedown Street* (1979) was (according to reviewer Gary Von Tersch) an "artistic dead end." To be fair, Lowell George was brilliant in his work with Little Feat, but was pretty far gone with his own demons by the time he sat in the control room to mix this album. He died soon afterward. One song on the album was already a Dead classic from the Pigpen era (a cover of the Rascals' "Good Lovin'") now redone with less energy as a Bob Weir number, while others would become staples in future Dead shows ("I Need a Miracle" and "Fire on the Mountain") but the record seemed lazy, as if the producer wanted to make a disco record and the band was pouting. The Dead had just returned from playing the Pyramids when they recorded this, so maybe they were still jetlagged. The very best thing about the album was its cover, drawn by Gilbert Shelton of *Fabulous Furry Freak Brothers* fame, who is, next to R. Crumb, the author's favorite comix artist. That was followed up by *Go to Heaven* (1980), which had the worst Dead album cover ever, a photo of the band in white leisure suits against a white, slightly foggy background. If the band refused to play disco, at least the record company would make them look like disco artists on the cover. Seriously, this cover design should've been reserved for KC and the Sunshine Band. On the vinyl itself, "Alabama Getaway" had some zip. The rest, like a lover whose consent terminates her participation, just lay there. The critics liked the Brent Mydland stuff the best, but to some he sounded like bad Doobie Brothers. (Brent, at eleven years, was keyboardist for the Dead longer than any other.) It would be seven years before the Dead released another studio album, this one *In the Dark*, which contained the band's first hit single, "Touch of Grey." Along with Top 40 fame and fortune at last, the album also seemed to signal a resurgence of Jerry as artistic director. He coproduced the record, and cowrote four of the seven songs. Bobby and Barlow kicked in with "Hell in a Bucket" and "Throwing Stones," the former offering a slogan, the second turning a deaf ear to hypocrisy (or certainly to irony) with its complaints about rich white men in their summer homes. During the Arista age, there wasn't a single noteworthy studio song that didn't appear on a live disc feeling more alive.

It was that old wheeze, Phoenix rising relentlessly from ashes.

25

THERE IS SUGAREE

Who is Sugaree? That's apparently in the ear of the beholder. When my wife became pregnant with our second child, son Matthew, we wanted to know as soon as possible the gender of the baby. For our first, our daughter Tekla, we asked that it be a surprise, and this turned out to be a mistake. Not knowing the gender was agonizing. We took to calling the fetus "Swee'pea," after the gender-uncertain baby in the Popeye cartoons. The mystery enabled us to have twice as many discussions about what to name the kid. I was certain that I wanted my daughter to be named Tekla, because I was and am convinced that the name is magic. She has to live a charmed life with a special name like that, and so far so good. The big argument was over the middle name. At one point, as one might expect, I suggested Tekla Sugaree Benson. My wife flared up as if I had just spit on the dining-room table.

"No way," she said.

"Why not?"

"Because Sugaree was a prostitute."

I was stunned speechless. She was? I had listened to the song, what, maybe two, three hundred times in my life, and though every version was different, I was fairly certain that Robert Hunter's lyrics had always remained the same; where did it say Sugaree was a prostitute?

I went to the source and examined the lyrics word by word and line by line. What did they tell us about the elusive heroine?

First, there would come a day when she would need to be taken down, to have her poor body dragged down, by persons arriving by wagon. I had always interpreted this to mean that Sugaree was not in good shape and her life expectancy was nil and she would die and need to be carted away. My wife saw this as an indication that Sugaree was a streetwalker and was subject to being rounded up by the paddy wagon. The guy singing the song, the story's narrator, wants to make sure Sugaree doesn't admit to knowing him, and that is admittedly some john/ho speak. Then Sugaree does the thing that trumps all other things—alas, she shakes it. Shakes it well, I've always believed. I saw a girl dancing in my mind. My wife saw the horizontal bop! Then the singer slams Sugaree, calls her out, how dare she have an ego? All of that acting cool, and perhaps the least of her problems is a severe case of insomnia. Maybe she was like Sweet Jane without the vitamin C. Maybe it was, "I'm a smart girl, I can do it and not get hooked." Since these things are happening despite all she's gained, then there must have been a successful portion of her life, back when shaking it was not as complex, perhaps as bittersweet, as it is at the time of the song. What good was that gain, the singer asks, when it didn't even provide shelter from a storm? If Sugaree is a whore, then the narrator knows her as more, for Sugaree is (like Ruby Tuesday in the Stones song) a slave to a voice that comes calling her, telling her it's time to move on. Or, she's in a whorehouse, and that voice is calling, "Next!" Maybe they'll see each other again at a biblical (Leviticus 25) party at which all debts are forgiven—or maybe they would cross paths as outlaws.

Just this superficial analysis illuminated part of Hunter's technique: No two people listening to the lyrics hear the same thing. The dots have been placed so far apart that we each connect them in our own way.

I wondered if there were any expert opinions. Oh my, are there.

Robert Reifenberg of Chicago said the song was "the plea of a fugitive American slave to his covert wife that she not reveal their relationship to the slave master." The wagon is the slave wagon. The jubilee is emancipation, and if they escape they would indeed be on the run. Excellent theory!

Hunter has some memories of writing the words from which we will cull clues. It wasn't cadged from Elizabeth Cotton's "Sugaree." Hunter's lyric was originally entitled "Stingaree," named after a poisonous South Sea manta. When writing the chorus Hunter recalled a time when he was broke and consorting with criminals, one of whom departed one day with the words, "Hold your mud and don't mention my name." The title was changed to Sugaree just because the word was more musical, and the name held exquisite irony for a hard-bitten woman.

Though the lyrics to Garcia/Hunter tunes are not similar to one another, the stories they tell all seem to be narrated by the same fellow, a man struggling in the lingering last vestiges of an outlaw tradition. The guy who wants to draw the queen of diamonds for an inside straight in "Loser," would seem to be the same guy who is asking Sugaree to keep their acquaintance secret, and the same guy who is down on the docks having a heart-to-heart with a wino. He likes to gamble, but he's not good at it, he likes women but he spends a lot of time on the move, he's a softie for a sad story, but he's up for a good time. Best guess is that guy is a little bit Robert and a little bit Jerry. Jerry told David Gans that Hunter always knew that he wouldn't sing a song if it made him feel like an idiot, that he was good at "writing into my beliefs." Rule number one, Hunter understood: Don't let that deal go down.

Bottom line: My daughter's middle initial isn't S.

26

THE COMMITMENT TO A CONCISE AESTHETIC AND TRADITIONAL SONG STRUCTURES

During the late 1960s, other San Francisco bands were charting singles and having their songs played on the AM radio. Jefferson Airplane did best, hitting the Top 10 twice during the Summer of Love (1967) with "Somebody to Love" and "White Rabbit," both off their pop-trippy album *Surrealistic Pillow*. Big Brother and the Holding Company, with lead singer Janis Joplin, went to number 12 on the Billboard Hot 100 with "Piece of My Heart" in the fall of 1968. Moby Grape and Quicksilver Messenger Service had minor hits with "Omaha" and "Fresh Air," respectively. And during all this the Grateful Dead were hardly ever played on the radio by anyone, ever. Lunar rotation at best. They weren't exactly unknown, their unusual name saw to that, but they were most famous for appearing in the lyrics to the titular song from the Broadway musical *Hair* and popularized on AM radio by the Cowsills: "It's not for lack of bread, / Like the Grateful Dead." With the coming of the 1970s, AM radio's Top 40 formats gave way to FM's progressive rock playlists, and the Dead responded by putting out a series of albums that were played in heavy rotation, well, from then on.

Maybe it was David Crosby's rap. Dave told Jerry that he believed the real art in music was creating songs that told stories.

Maybe it started when Jerry rediscovered the piano. He'd played as a small child, switched to banjo and then guitar as a young man, and didn't go back—until 1969–70, when Jerry sat down to plunk the ivories and liked the feel so much he took to writing songs.

The Dead albums to debut in 1970 were *Workingman's Dead* and *American Beauty*. The next year brought *Grateful Dead* (a double live album—with plentiful overdubs—best known as *Skull and Roses*). Up until those albums, the Dead had not made a popular record. Their first record was done on dexies, and they played even the long songs so fast that they didn't last three minutes. *Anthem of the Sun*, the second album, reminded some of a Disney movie in which live action and animation function side by side on the screen. They made recordings of songs played live and in the studio, and overlaid them to form a hybrid, then mixed the result down and down into excessive weirdness. For *Aoxomoxoa*, so named because the word is a palindrome, the group decided to record the way the real pros did, one track at a time, and that quickly became too fragmentary, simply not "group" enough. Jerry experimented with filtering his vocals through a variety of devices, phasers, to create a trippy effect, one that would set a trend and show up even on AM radio in a few months.

And then, for one brief shining moment, they got their act together and produced back-to-back their two finest studio LPs: *Workingman's Dead* and *American Beauty*.

When *Workingman's Dead* was released, all you had to do was look at the cover art to tell the band was taking a new direction. Gone were the colorful psychedelic swirls, replaced by a grainy sepia tone of the band standing on a street corner, looking for all the world like members of a casual labor pool waiting for the van to come. The songs on that record were concise, told of men who busted up rocks and worked in the mines, and laden with contagious musical hooks.

Plus, there was a new emphasis on vocal harmonies. The Dead during this time had become great admirers of Crosby, Stills &

Nash's sound, and these tunes reflected that. Steven Stills was living at the time on Mickey Hart's ranch, and David Crosby had Jerry's ear, so there was a new feeling in the studio that the human voice was the holiest of all instruments. Instead of thinking louder, the band thought prettier and grittier, with stunning results. *Rolling Stone* readers voted *Workingman's Dead* the best album of 1970.

The question now became, what do the Dead do for an encore? Turned out they had that covered. Only months later they released *American Beauty*, a recording of great tranquility—but when it came to recording it, being tranquil had nothing to do with it. Members of the Dead were grieving during its making. Phil's dad died of cancer. Jerry's mom was in a horrific car accident in the Twin Peaks section of San Francisco, and lingered in San Francisco General for a while before she expired.* The whole band had to deal with a blow-up with a manager over big-time embezzlement and the New Orleans drug bust immortalized in the lyrics of "Truckin'." (According to Phil, those under arrest were dragged to jail, at first all in one tank, then to individual cells, and somehow during this process Bobby managed to handcuff a cop to his own chair.) Some of the songs came easy, others like pulling teeth. "Ripple" practically emerged from the guitar without human assistance (during the Festival Express train ride across Canada), Jerry didn't even feel like he had anything to do with it. Hunter wrote a haiku chorus and it was immediately far out. On the other hand, the previously mentioned "Truckin'" was a labor, with the whole band in on the creative process. The song has great changes, hit-single-worthy hooks, but it made for a puzzle that, at first any-

---

*Jerry was glad that his mom had had an opportunity to see the Grateful Dead, to see what all of the fuss was about regarding her son. Jerry played for his mom at a show at the Rock Garden, in the Mission district of San Francisco, in 1967. Jerry could tell she liked it. She asked, "Jerry, how do you get your guitar to sound like a horn like that?" She was so far out.

way, was difficult to assemble. "Box of Rain" was the first *American Beauty* song to be written, and it occupied the coveted side-one, cut-one position on the vinyl disk. It was created in a different way from most Dead songs: Phil wrote the music first, and Hunter fit the lyric to it, note by note, syllable by syllable.

The two 1970 studio masterpieces were recorded at Wally Heider's new studio in the Tenderloin section of San Francisco on Hyde Street between Turk and Eddy. The facility had three studios in it. There were supposed to be four but the fourth was never built and became the game room, another reason the Dead liked it there. Even when your studio time was through you could still hang out, and there were always other musicians there, CSN&Y, Paul Kantner and Grace Slick of the Airplane, Carlos Santana, and others. The social scene was excellent, and you never had to go far to find a guest musician. "Anyone play a dobro?"

With the fresh batch of studio excellence, the Dead's repertoire had gone from spacey free-form to the countrified rock 'n' roll sound (good ol' Grateful Dead) that they'd retain in large part from then on. Recorded in 1971 and released in January 1972, Jerry added to the songbook, writing with Hunter and on a piano, with a new solo LP called *Garcia* that gave us "Deal," "Sugaree," "Loser," and "The Wheel."* Also in 1972 Bobby released *Ace*, which now sounds like a greatest-hits compilation: "Greatest Story Ever Told," "Black-Throated Wind," "Playing in the Band," "Looks Like Rain," "Mexicali Blues," "One More Saturday Night," and "Cassidy."

Though the Dead never gave up completely on the acidy sound —every concert continued to have a trippy interlude—they now had songs that were perfectly suited for singing along and dancing:

---

*While Jerry was working on a solo project, Bobby lost both of his adoptive parents within a week. In a truly bizarre coincidence, Bobby's dad died on his mom's birthday, and his mom died on his dad's birthday.

"Uncle John's Band," "Cumberland Blues," and "Casey Jones" from *Workingman's Dead*; "Friend of the Devil," "Sugar Magnolia," and "Truckin'" from *American Beauty*; and "Bertha," "Playing in the Band," "Wharf Rat," and "Not Fade Away/Goin' Down the Road Feeling Bad" from *Grateful Dead*. Everyone forgot about the lyrics to "Hair." For the first time, the Dead had records everyone wanted to buy.

For the rest of their days, the Dead would hope for another studio album with half the mastery of their 1970 LPs. But it didn't happen, and Bobby had as good of a theory as anyone. Because of the Beatles, it became traditional for bands to put on their new record their latest songs, penned or arranged by themselves. Trouble was, this band needed to air songs out a little bit before they could master them. Rare was the new song that wasn't played stiffly, and those were the performances you heard on Dead studio albums. Bobby said they should have made a rule that they weren't allowed to play a song in the studio until they'd toured with it for a while to discover what secrets it held.

As a footnote, all of the FM airplay in the world did nothing to help the Dead get a hit single until 1987. Bobby famously claimed that the single "Truckin'" went to number 1 in Turlock, California, but this has proven impossible to verify. Nationally, it only made it to number 64 in January 1971, nowhere near high enough to get it AM airplay—and for some reason "Johnny B. Goode" was the A-side, with "Truckin'" on the flip. The song did, however, fuel a million high-school yearbook quotes over the next decade.

27

WHEN YOUTH WAS GOD, JERRY PLAYED OLD

The Dead rose to fame during a time when the youth movement had never been stronger. The baby boomers were so plentiful that they felt they could take over. Don't trust anyone over thirty, was *the* famous slogan of the '60s. The Who hoped they died before they got old, and some of them did. There was a 1968 movie called *Wild in the Streets* in which a James Dean–wannabe named Christopher Jones played a leader of a rock band who gains significant political influence with his call for voting rights for teenagers. Jerry and Pigpen bought into *none* of this. Jerry knew the value of things that were old, that there was wisdom to be gained from his elders and previous generations. He had his maternal grandmother to thank for that. Jerry's dad died when he was young and he spent a lot of time living with Grandma, whose personality did much to shape her grandson. She was a radical and organized labor unions, but she listened to music that provided a history lesson of America: bluegrass, folk, and blues. Every Saturday night she and little Jerry would turn on the radio and listen to the Grand Ole Opry. The Dead were antiwar, of course, and generally endorsed Democrats over Republicans, but they never recorded a protest song. "One More Saturday Night" takes a gentle stab at the weapons of war. The closest they came to a protest song was in "Mountains of the Moon," which uses images of world conflict as examples of how we are not sticking together as earthlings, a strategy that would be obvious if you were looking at the earth from the moon's perspective. Their political message was simply be kind to each other and to your planet.

28

OF THE ART

Whereas Dead music was eclectic, the visual artwork that accompanied their posters, LP covers, and T-shirts took a remarkably specific thematic approach. Lettering swirls and drips, electric Day-Glo colors vibrate kaleidoscopically, and the images are of roses, human bones, and happy dancing bears. There was a turtle phase around *Terrapin*, but it went away.

The style was solidly in place by 1966—with hard-to-read posters, letters so much a part of the busy design as to be almost illegible—long before the whole world went psychedelic, affecting the design of mainstream TV, from the sets of *Rowan and Martin's Laugh-In*, to the Partridge family's bus.

Because of their link with the band, talented artists whose fame might have faded along with the psychedelic era—Stanley Mouse (born Stanley George Miller), Alton Kelley, Victor Moscoso, David Singer, et al.—are still popular, their work displayed in museums, and sold at auction.

Mouse came from Detroit, and spent some time painting Rat Finks on hot rods before, as a member of the Family Dog, he took part in producing some early Dead shows. It was in the Family Dog that Mouse met Alton Kelley, a self-taught artist from Nevada. The most enduring image from the Dead art collection is not an original painting but rather a repurposing of an existing image—much like the best known of Andy Warhol's work. The image—a human skeleton wearing a crown of roses, holding a wreath of roses in its left hand and picking flowers from a rose-bush with its right—was originally drawn by British illustrator Edmund J. Sullivan and published as an illustration in a 1900 edition of Omar Khayyam's *Rubaiyat*, but was repurposed by Mouse and Kelley first as a poster advertising the Dead's September 16 and 17, 1966, shows at the Avalon Ballroom, and eventually and most famously as the cover of the 1971 double LP officially called *Grateful Dead*, but forever to be remembered as *Skull and Roses*.

Dead artwork is not limited to paintings, posters, and T-shirts. Jake Martin from my hometown of Rochester, New York, runs a jewelry company called Dupree's Diamond Dealer that exclusively makes jam-band jewelry, of which the majority is Dead themed. His slogan is: "Handmade jewelry. For heads, by heads." And every piece they sell really is handmade right there in their Rochester shop in the Hungerford Building, a big old warehouse divvied up into spaces for artists of all stripes to make and sell their wares. He was eighteen when he started making jewelry. He took a jewelry-making class at a community college and knew right away that this was for him. At the time, when he wasn't going to school, he was following RatDog from show to show, so the first pieces he made were all Jerry with wings. He's twenty-six now, which means he was six when Jerry passed away, a member of the new generation of Deadheads that don't see Dead World as nostalgic* but rather as *classic*—a then version of something that still exists now.

*A lot of bands spend only a short time being active, popular, and creative, and then they fall back on that period for their income for decades. A good example is the Beach Boys—Mike Love's version of the Beach Boys, anyway, not so much Brian Wilson's. The Dead created new songs every time they appeared on stage. They were certainly never a nostalgia act. And, while it's true that some members of their audiences grew older, and that by the 1990s it was not uncommon to see gray ponytails swinging back and forth out there, the bulk of the audience stayed the same age. The Deadhead community was constantly

Once he realized he could make a living by selling jewelry, first in the parking lot outside shows and eventually online, his fate was sealed, and thankfully sales have been brisk. He thinks his success hinges not just on loving the subject matter but on understanding the wants and needs of the niche he's filling. Dead-oriented artwork has been subtly changed and modified over the years, but it stringently adheres to a certain look that is far more classical and approachable than it would be were Martin creating his own contemporary designs. The style he uses today was popular ten years ago and will be ten years from now. He doesn't have to worry about—and he hates this word with a passion—what's *fashionable* today in the jam-band community.

"For older fans, they see the Dead as an outgrowth of a counter-culture, but for fans my age it isn't that anymore, it is a culture in and of itself, and the people within it are so diverse that it absorbs new influences all the time. Everything changes except the look. That's classic."

---

turning over, yet maintaining homeostasis: old members taking themselves off the road to settle down and get on with the seriousness of life, while new teenagers and twenty-somethings climbed aboard.

THE CONCERT FILMS

Of their concert films, the most noteworthy by far is *The Grateful Dead Movie* (1977), directed by Jerry. Multiple cameras filmed a five-night run of 1974 concerts at Winterland, the band in its full Wall of Sound glory, along with excited and stoned activities in and around the arena before and during the shows. It is one of the great concert movies, a superior documentary that immortalized the words, "There is nothing like a Grateful Dead concert."

Rock Scully finds it one of the great injustices of the Dead's history that Jerry spent two and a half years editing this movie, pouring his soul into it, synching up the sound to the image, getting it perfect, and the rest of the band didn't seem to notice, and when they did notice they mostly complained. It contains a complex cartoon sequence of a sort that had never before been attempted. Scully thinks the tragedy of Jerry was that he lost touch with his brothers, and with the real world, only after his brothers lost touch with him.

Everybody's favorite scene was the laughing-gas party, a circle of freaks around a metallic dentist's hookah, with octopus tubes for inhaling the nitrous oxide, and a device that stopped the gas flow automatically if you lost your grip and let go of the nozzle. There's that guy who's stuck outside. He's supposed to be on the list, but he isn't—and later you see him inside dancing happily in front of the stage. There's Phil using the movie camera and his bass to achieve feedback like a mad aural scientist. It's a classic, and a lot of it was Jerry's work.

The movie took its time getting to New York, but when it did it became a regular "midnight movie," at theaters with top-notch sound systems and balconies where you could smoke, where I saw it abundantly, and fell asleep during "Morning Dew" (near the end) every time.

The Grateful Dead Movie was shown in a one-night-only rerelease in 540 movie theaters on April 20, 2011, thirty-four years after its debut. The event was so successful that they did it again a few weeks later. The rerelease not only made money, but parents took their kids and helped create a whole new generation of fans.

There are other movies: *Grateful Dead So Far* (1987); *Grateful Dead: The Closing of Winterland* (2003); *Sunshine Daydream* (2013), film of a 1972 concert in Oregon. Their songs have appeared in the soundtracks to many Hollywood movies (*Runaway Bride, Zabriskie Point, The Dreamers, The Box, The Twilight Zone*, for example), they're on hundreds of YouTube videos, and now, Martin Scorsese is on board, planning a documentary film!

And there is *Festival Express* (2003), which documents the real-life adventures of the Dead, Janis, the Band and others who in 1970, post-Woodstock, traveled across Canada by railroad, playing a series of concerts. The film was not known so much for its shows, although Janis was particularly good at one of them, but for the party that was going on in the train as it crossed the thousands of miles from Montreal to Vancouver. It was technically called the Trans-Canada Festival Express, and it was supposed to be like a traveling Woodstock. It would be wrong to say that the Festival was a success—turns out there weren't that many hippies in Canada—but the film certainly is. Jerry's funny. Too drunk to walk, he can still play guitar unaffected. Ten days, five scheduled shows (one canceled), individual sleeping compartments and *two* bar cars. When the booze on the train ran out there was an unscheduled stop and the musicians passed the hat and bought out a small-town liquor store in the middle of the night. So much fun. Oh, the hangovers.

The Scorsese project has Deadheads excited, not only because Scorsese has been associated with great concert films in the past (*The Last Waltz*; *George Harrison: Living in the Material World*; *Shine a Light*) but because it will be directed by Amir Bar-Lev, and contain never-before-seen footage from the Dead's vaults.

A press release from 2014 quotes Scorsese as saying, "The Grateful Dead were more than just a band. They were their own planet, populated by millions of devoted fans. I'm very happy that the picture is being made and proud to be involved."

Bar-Lev said, "It's been ten years since I first set out to make a film about the Grateful Dead, and I'm thrilled that it's finally happening."

The music is being chosen by archivist David (*Dave's Picks*) Lemieux.

The release, made available on www.dead.net, concluded with a joint statement from the Dead's surviving members: "Millions of stories have been told about the Grateful Dead over the years. With our fiftieth anniversary coming up, we thought it might just be time to tell one ourselves and Amir is the perfect guy to help us do it. Needless to say, we are humbled to be collaborating with Martin Scorsese."

The band was changed forever by their drummers' participation in Francis Ford Coppola's *Apocalypse Now*, in 1979. Mickey was really the one in charge. While planning out the soundtrack, Mickey instilled in himself a heart of darkness. When he heard sounds in his head, he had to invent the instrument to make those sounds. Eventually, all of those invented instruments went on the road with the Dead and form what's called "The Beast"—the array of percussion instruments hung from a metal frame at the rear of the set.

30

THEIR MUSIC IS SO FLEXIBLE

Grateful Dead songs can be simple enough to be played by a beginning acoustic guitar player sitting on a bench in a park, and complex enough to be arranged for a philharmonic orchestra. They've been covered by jazz bands, performed a cappella, played with a reggae beat, and perhaps most impressively presented as classical composition.

The relationship between the Dead and the black-tie set dates back to 1970, right around the time they were making their two most beautiful studio albums. It was a time when Bobby was stepping up his game as a guitarist, finally outgrowing the "he's got potential" phase, and now fully realizing his slightly goofy vision of what a rhythm guitarist is and could be. He also locked into his role as the guy who snaps the band back to reality when its orbit around the earth gets just a little bit too eccentric.

On March 17, 1970, the Grateful Dead performed at Kleinhans Music Hall in Buffalo, New York, with the Buffalo Philharmonic Orchestra (BPO). For years there had been a lot of talk about this performance but the details remained "mysterious-yet-legendary" until Buffalonian Deadhead Jay Gerland rooted out the facts in 2004.

The BPO was unhelpful, having retained no program or photographs from the events—or memories, apparently. Research on the Dead side was also in vain. The master vault didn't have a record of the show. (Owsley wasn't allowed to travel at the time of the

Buffalo show because of a drug bust, and that's probably the reason no one bothered to record it. Owsley later said he would have recorded it had he been there because he recorded everything.)

Gerland had better luck with the *Buffalo Evening News* archives at the Buffalo Public Library, and a fellow he knew named Steve Waltman, in seventh grade at the time, had clipped out the review of the hybrid performance in the next day's *Buffalo Courier-Express*, a newspaper that is long-defunct—so at least we have proof that it actually occurred. Gerland eventually found a BPO percussionist named Lynn Harbold who joined Bill and Mickey for that evening's "Drums."

The concert was more than a musical experiment, but meant to be a salve for a particularly rough period in Buffalo's history, as antiwar protests at the University of Buffalo had turned violent only days before and there had been multiple arrests.

The warm-up band at the show was western New York's the Yellow Brick Road. A preview of the show in the *Evening News* said that the Dead's portion of the program was part of the "Philharmonic Rock Marathon." The Dead, the paper said, were filling in for the Byrds, who had been a late scratch.

The show that night was conducted by Lukas Foss, the BPO's musical director from 1963 to 1971, who'd been a child prodigy in Germany, fled the Nazis, and was known for his "experiments in performance," most notably by his Improvisation Chamber Ensemble, which performed pieces with titles like "Time Space." Foss and Garcia/Lesh, it would seem, were a match made in heaven, or some equivalent location of raised consciousness.

The Dead, the preview noted, had waved their usual "huge fee" and were there for the "privilege and delight" of working with Foss. History would be made during the four-hour, six-part show, as it was the first ever fully shared concert by a philharmonic and a rock band. There was also to be a "far-out light show" on the music hall's walls created by a $4,000—insert Dr. Evil scare quotes —"laser and prism machine." The show began with Foss on piano and the Dead in support for a non-improvisational version of the Bach "Concerto in F Minor." (I'm having trouble imagining Bob Weir getting through this piece without improvising just a little bit. Just sayin'.) The Dead would then play an hour set on their own, followed by a BPO/Dead debut performance of the Foss composition "Geod," with "laser" show. The Dead would play another forty-minute set, then all musicians on stage, Foss conducting, for a performance of John Cage's "Variations II and III." The night would conclude with a massive "musical challenge jam session."

That was what was supposed to happen. What actually happened, music critic James Brennan wrote, was so magical that the preshow ground rules became meaningless. The Dead, after all, went into even the most rehearsed situations, which this wasn't, with only a modicum of arrangement for their songs. Dead songs were charted by outsiders, not by the Dead. As Jerry told David Gans, "The intraband collaboration is almost total, insofar as that's what a song is in the Grateful Dead—a melody, lyrics, and chord changes, and that's it. Apart from that, it's what everybody finds to say."

In Buffalo, there was "a sound that sent a sublime shock" through the music hall, an "extraordinary rapport between the Dead's rock and the orchestral prose." The Dead, we learn, played "Dark Star" and Pigpen sang "Love Night" (probably "Turn on Your Love Light" misheard). The Dead, Brennan concluded, fared better in the experiment than did the Yellow Brick Road: "The Grateful Dead worked their wave of music more adeptly around this free-form style with a lot more adroit ramifications."

Gerland found a guy named Don Lesser, then a student at SUNY Fredonia, who *went to the show* with four friends. A woman in the hallway was handing out pink tabs of acid.

"Someone gave these to me and told me to hand them out," she said.

Turned out to be excellent stuff.

The Yellow Brick Road sucked. They were a "teeny-bopper band." Once the acid kicked in, Lesser's reportage becomes less trustworthy, but he believes the laser show projected "four oscilloscope roses, red, green, blue, and yellow, that swelled and changed with the music." (Thomas Putnam, writing for the *Courier-Express*, saw no flowers, and said they were "circular forms.")

Eventually the group of college kids moved up to the front where Jerry had stopped playing songs and was "playing the pulse of the room." Bobby's eyes were going in different directions. They asked him if he wanted to come back to Fredonia with them and he said no thanks, he had to go back to the hotel.

"In the second half, the orchestra was split in two sections, the Yellow Brick Road was in the front left and the Dead were in the front right. Lukas Foss, the Philharmonic director, led them on some orchestral space music, pointing to different sections of the musicians to have the music rise and fall."

The John Cage piece, it seemed, included a lecture by John Cage during which the musicians wandered around the audience. Everyone agrees that the audience, at some point, became part of the show, adding their own "knocking and popping" noises to the jam. Foss was criticized for continuing to conduct even as the musicians wanted to improvise, resorting to verbal cues, like "Attack! . . . gliss downward! . . . vibrato!"

Overall, however, everyone had a great time, and, according to Brennan, "as an evening of rock and symphony avant-garde it was not only entertaining and often exciting, but carved new territory for players and listeners in both styles."

Too bad no one turned on a tape recorder.

Two other noteworthy intersections of the Dead and a classical orchestra occurred more recently, one in August 2009 commemorating the fourteenth anniversary of Jerry's death, the other May 2012, the common denominator being a fellow named Lee Johnson, who charts Dead songs for classical performance.

The first was a performance of the twelve-movement *Dead Symphony no. 6* by the Cabrillo Festival Orchestra in Santa Cruz, conducted by Marin Alsop. The same piece had first been recorded by the Russian National Orchestra and released on CD in 2007. It rather thrillingly broke the mold of lame attempts to play popular music in a classical setting. Ever hear the string quartet version of Paul McCartney's "Maybe I'm Amazed"? No? Well, good.

The Dead symphony wasn't just an adaptation, it used Dead tunes as a launching point for original musical riffs, which of course is what the Dead used them for as well. The songs referenced included "Mountains of the Moon," "Stella Blue," and "Sugar Magnolia." The orchestra even warmed up with Luigi Denza's "Funiculi Funicula," to better mimic a Dead performance.

The show was, in a way, a thank you to the Dead, whose charity work had helped fund the preservation of composer Lou Harrison's archives at UC Santa Cruz. When he was a kid, Jerry's family vacationed in Santa Cruz, so it was always one of his favorite places.

During the summer of 2009, Lee Johnson donated the score for *Dead Symphony no. 6* to UCSC's special collections.

Dead publicist and biographer Dennis McNally isn't surprised that a classical performance of Dead songs could garnish so much respect from classical fans. "People forget how finely composed the songs are. There's an underlying beauty to their structure and content that makes them malleable to be recast," McNally says.

For the 2012 show, the Susquehanna Symphony Orchestra, under the direction of Sheldon Bair, and accompanied by twenty-two all-county orchestra students, took on *Dead no. 6*. Here the musicians dropped their formal attire and wore instead matching tie-dyed T-shirts. The audience loved it, and everyone agreed it was a strange but fitting conclusion to the SSO's thirty-fifth season.

And let's not forget the Dark Star Orchestra, which isn't an orchestra at all but rather a Dead cover band that doesn't just cover Dead songs, but since 1997 entire Dead shows, playing precise covers of complete playlists. Playing two hundred shows a year, the DSO has counted among its guest musicians Bobby, Phil, Bill, Donna Jean, Vince Welnick, and Tom Constanten.

The Dead's music is so supple, in fact, that there is a disagreement over when they are or aren't playing music. Which leads me to a story.

My wife—then my girlfriend—was in law school, which puts this in the mid-1980s, and I was visiting her apartment. There was a live Dead show being broadcast on the radio. It might've been New Year's Eve. The band was late taking the stage—"there's a problem with Jerry" we were told—and when they got on stage they tuned up forever before noodling their way into the first song. The tuning went on for so long that the local radio station DJ felt obliged to break in and inform listeners of what was happening. The guy simply said, "The Grateful Dead: they tune because they love." Now, I never minded the Dead tuning up. There were nights when tuning was better than "Space." So it didn't shock me when I learned that Dead fan David Murphy took master tapes of some of the Dead's best 1977 shows and compiled ninety minutes of *just* tuning. He called it *Tuning '77*, which is a cool name. He didn't call it "They Tune Because They Love" because he probably wasn't listening to the Long Island radio station Lisa and I had tuned into that night. Murphy admitted to *Rolling Stone* magazine that most people don't make it through the full ninety minutes. He says, "It's a conceptual art piece. It's an audio piece that is really about the idea of what does sound sound like when no music is happening." Conceptual artists simply don't pull this shit with bands that don't matter.

OF THE FORTY-FIVE-MINUTE "SUGAREE"

It was summer vacation between my third and fourth years of college, 1977, and, drinking way too much, I had this haunting feeling that the 1960s were relevant but the 1970s were not—haunting because I felt like I'd been born too late, forced to watch all the good stuff on TV as a kid. I was desperate to get some of that relevance under my belt.*

We were three years past the fall of Saigon, one year past the country's oddly joyless bicentennial celebration, and behind us as we headed west, in New York City, there would be the Summer of Sam dominated by a .44 Bulldog, and the summer of the blackout with its subsequent looting and burning, bad news I read about in the newspapers like all other out-of-towners.

Nick and I, each nursing broken hearts involving fickle co-eds, were heading west looking for Jerry, neo-hippies, sick of the plasticity of the disco era, and filled with rosy visions of the Summer of Love and free love and organic music. Maybe like Steve Winwood's "Dear Mr. Fantasy," Jerry would make us happy with his non-straight mind.

We hopped into Nick's rusted-out dark-green Pinto hatchback (blissfully unaware that it would later become known as the most

---

*Although this is a true-ish story, some names and locations have been changed to protect the privacy of the innocent.

dangerous automobile in history) and, with $200 and a cassette case full of homegrown between us, headed west. Every gas station was manned by what Nick called "guardian angels," Jesus freaks in white overalls giving us the "one way" gesture along with the gas and clean windshield. We were run around by a couple of high-school girls in Chicago, got drunk in an all-black bar in Denver, and narrowly escaped shack-dwelling psychos outside Salt Lake City, all the time singing "Gotta get down to the Cumberland miiiines."

For us the Grateful Dead were a recorded thing. I had *Workingman's Dead* and *American Beauty*, *Skull and Roses*, and a live recording of an Avalon Ballroom show from 1966 put out under the title *Vintage Dead*, and purchased from the cutout bin. We had totally bought into the Captain Trips/guru scam, because it was written on a Jefferson Airplane album cover and that meant it had to be true. But we'd never seen the Dead in person—and as neophytes who missed that stuff, we didn't know from "Dark Star." We were more like, "Second one is prison, baby, sheriff's on my trail." The last time the Dead played in my hometown I was too young. Weir and Kingfish came to my college the previous year and that was great, I liked a good cowboy tune—but it wasn't the whole deal, and I knew it.

The Pinto was on its last legs and unprepared for the challenges presented by the Continental Divide. It cleared the Rockies with great protest and broke down for good in Lovelock, Nevada, so we bought Greyhound tickets to San Francisco, and found accommodations in a rundown Market Street hotel called the National, where the clientele was mostly young and lost. Nick got a job selling stuff on the phone, and I worked for the U.S. Postal Service of San Francisco "throwing paper," that is, putting advertisements in people's mailboxes in hilly Frisco, Oakland, San Jose, and Concord.

In Concord there was a brush fire up on a mountain and firefighters in helicopters were pouring purple dust on it.

Survival took up most of our time. We'd visited Haight-Ashbury, and of course found the Summer of Love to be ten years gone. We talked to those who'd been there and were told it never really happened, just a construct of the media. Ninety percent of free love turned out to be rape. The rest was prostitution, not free at all.

The only thing left on our list was organic music, and we were pleased to find that it was real, and it was still around. We hung around outside Wally Heider's, every once in a while seeing a celeb. Mick Fleetwood, busy making *Rumours*, asked me what was going down.

Then it got really good, starting in the beginning of August when I spotted an ad in the *Bay-Guardian* newspaper: "Appearing To-Nite: The Jerry Garcia Band." I tore the ad out of the paper and shoved it into the back pocket of my patched Levis.

I asked Nick: "How do we get there?" I'd been to Berkeley throwing paper but going and coming I was in the back of a windowless box truck.

"I know where to find out," Nick said. "The tourist information center!" It wasn't really a center, just a kiosk really, like a concession stand, only all they had were pamphlets. It was located at the base of the Civic Center's giant wall.

"Excuse me, how do we get to the Keystone Club in Berkeley, Miss?" I asked the girl in the booth. She knew what tourists liked and was wearing a tie-dyed summer dress.

"Keystone Berkeley? F Bus takes you right there," she said. "Catch it at the Transbay Bus Station."

"Who's playing?" she asked.

"Garcia."

"Far out," she said. "Keystone is general admission. The earlier you get there the better your seats'll be."

"Thanks."

"What about advance sales? Do they sell tickets ahead of time?"

Nick asks. Oooh, good question. Don't want to get to the Keystone Club and find the concert's been sold out for three weeks.

"I don't think they sell in advance, you'd better call and find out," the girl says.

We thank her again and find a pay phone. Nick drops the dime and I read the number off the ad. Nick finds out that tickets are first come, first served. Doors open at seven. That's when tickets go on sale. It's one in the afternoon now.

"He said we should get there early. They are expecting a big crowd," Nick says.

"Let's leave now. That way we can be front row center," I say, and we're off to the bus station. Across the Bay Bridge and I can see the forest fire on the Concord mountain. Still burning. Same old choppers circling the smoke, dropping ground-up purple micro-dot. Bus turns north.

Must be getting close to a college town now. There's a guy ped-aling a six-foot unicycle outside the window, eye level with us. We give him big thumbs up.

Sure enough, the bus lets us off right at the Keystone. The place is yellow with a big red painted sign up above. No bigger than a saloon. JGB is Jerry's saloon band. There's no one else around. Five hours till the doors open. Sun beating hard. Not a cloud in the sky. It'll never cease to amaze me how hot it can be on one side of the Bay and so cold on the other.

Nick takes off looking for alcohol. I pull out the copy of *Melody Maker* I bought at the Frisco bus station and start to read. I sit cross-legged on the sidewalk. The magazine is convinced that punk rock is a threat to the internal stability of Great Britain. Get a grip, says I. Just then the front door to the club opens and a big sleepy-eyed blond dude is standing there. I'm startled. Hadn't thought anyone was around.

"You first in line?" he asks, squinting out into the daylight.

"That's me."

He laughs a little. He's wearing a denim jacket with the sleeves cut off, no shirt underneath. A series of vans drive by, all adorned by Rat Fink van art. Must be some sort of Rat Fink club. Then there're three convertibles all in a row, each with a lone driver, that being a sun-tanned stud in reflective sunglasses. Then the parade is over, gone as quickly as it came.

"How many does this place hold?" I ask.

"Four-hunnerd-fifty." He's rubbing at one eye with a greasy forefinger. I'm thinking that he might have slept in the club. Perhaps the Keystone is his home.

"How are the acoustics?"

"Perfect. It's the only place around here Jerry'll play."

"Decent. Can I take a peek?"

"Sure." He turns around—and I can see the Hells Angels logo on his back. Oakland chapter. I follow him through the double doors and into the theater. The place is so dark that it takes time for my eyes to adjust.

The first thing I can see is the stage, to the left of the entrance. Backstage can't actually be in back of the stage, because the street is there. It must run along one of the sidewalls, or it was all the way in the back, just like the clubhouses in the old Polo Grounds were in center field. There's a balcony. It hangs low and comes close to the stage in the front. Like the theater where Ed Sullivan did his show. On the main floor there are round tables around the perimeter and a large open space in the middle. The dance floor. The wood smells beer-soaked. There's still a blue haze of last night's smoke.

"The best seats are in the front of the balcony. That's where the sound really comes together," he says. "You get up close and you have to stand up all the time. Little dude like you won't see a fucking thing."

Nick comes back with the world's biggest bottle of apricot

brandy. He has been for quite a hike to find the liquor store and doesn't want attitude.

"This is going to get us awfully drunk, you know," I say, pulling out the cork and taking a swig. I wince as it bites my tongue and throat then sigh as my innards warm. "Good though." And we get way too drunk.

In about a half hour the Hells Angel reemerges from the Keystone and we're really pleased to see him. "Hey, don't get caught with that open bottle. Nobody from in here is going to hassle you," he says, "but if Berkeley cops catch you, they'll pop you. They'd rather see you blowing weed than having a beer or whatever that shit is you're drinking. Beats me why."

"Want some?" Nick says.

The biker shrugs, pulls the cork, glugs twice, wipes his mouth with his hand and says, "You dudes are gonna get fucked up. You'll be cool, right? Just don't rub the pig's nose in it."

"We'll be cool," I say.

"Could we have a couple paper cups?" Nick asks.

"Naw, man. Cups all got Keystone on 'em. Hot dog place across the street'll give you cups. I don't give a shit as long as it's got nothing to do with the club."

"What's your name?"

"I'm Ricky," he says. We introduce ourselves. Real names. Nick and I give Ricky's greasy thumb a good squeeze.

Nick crosses the street and comes back with two large cups filled with ice. It's about three o'clock when a blonde lady who came out of nowhere stops in front of the club wearing too much lipstick. Hey, she's looking at us. Snap to.

"You're here for Jerry, I see," she says, very London private-school posh.

"Oh yes, really looking forward to it," I say. My words are still not slurred.

"And how many times for you is this?" she asks.

"First time," I say. "From back East where he isn't too often."

"Oh dear," she says, forlorn at the thought. "I guess we are blessed to have him so frequently. I've seen him some thirty-odd times. Frankly I've been disappointed by him lately."

"He's someone I must see."

"Oh most assuredly," she says. "I've seen him both with the Dead and the band—his band not the Band . . ."

"No, I know . . . "

"Have you seen *The Dead Movie*?"

"No, but I read they're only booking it into theaters with adequate sound systems."

"You absolutely *must* see it! The only problem is that it never seems to stick around for very long. I think there are only five or six copies in distribution around North America. It was in town for five or six days, I believe, and then it was gone. Must be moving on now. It really has been a pleasure chatting." And she bounces down the street.

The equipment truck shows up and the roadies haul the shit through a utility door just the far side of the people entrance, in the direction of the Berkeley campus. Three of the roadies are also Angels.

Ricky calls them over and tells them about Nick and me, the ridiculous hour at which we arrived, and what I have hidden under my denim jacket. So they come over, say, hey, little dude, and each take a swig off the bottle.

I ask who's going to be in the band and they say Maria Muldaur is going to be singing backup alongside Donna Jean, and that Ron Tutt is drumming. John Kahn usually plays bass so he probably is. That's all they know. Sometimes Jerry doesn't know who all is playing until the show starts.

The line starts to grow at five o'clock. The third person in line is a lump of sugar about five foot two with a mop of curly hair and a Little Orphan Annie face. She almost immediately hits on Nick.

While they sit on the sidewalk and talk with their foreheads close together I finish the bottle. Twice I have to stagger down to the corner gas station to piss. Walking is hard. Thinking is harder.

Paranoia sets in. This is a club that serves alcohol. All of the cups have Keystone on them. They are going to be checking ID at the door. I am, at age twenty, sunk. You can drink at eighteen in New York, very civilized. Nick says he will give me a piece of his ID and then move further back in line.

"With people going by so fast they'll never figure out that there are two Nicholas Vallones in the crowd," Nick says.

"My eyes are blue."

"They'll never notice. It's dark in there."

For the first time I see that all of the equipment, including the truck, has "Property of the Grateful Dead" written on it. The roadies are big, There are six of them I think. Six or seven. Four are wearing Angels colors. The line has grown long behind us, all hairy hippies, a river of patched denim. The Angels now have their own booze. Jack. None of the movers of equipment is Ricky. There is probably a second crew working at the stage. Maybe he is one of them.

The roadies are crude with women as they pass. A guy with a wide-brimmed cowboy hat saunters by, his fingertips inside the tops of his jeans and, in a repetitive and rhythmic voice says, "Acid. Jerry G Acid. Acid. Jerry G Acid."

"Hey," Nick says.

Shelley says she doesn't do acid after it French fried her cousin. She doesn't so Nick doesn't. I am first in line and thinking that sustaining consciousness is about to become a full-time job when the doors open and it's Ricky standing there. "Single file," he barks and everyone pushes forward instead of backing up. Ricky gives up on single file. He retreats back inside, the doors now propped open and yells, "Have your IDs out boys and girls."

I follow him in and am ready with Nick's ID.

"Hey, little dude!" he says, pleased to see that I have retained the number-one position. I deserve it. Ricky barely glances at the ID and points me toward the ticket window. Give money, get stamped. A blue skeleton key on the back of my right hand. The place looks a lot bigger than it did when I was sober. The stage is filled with sound equipment and wire—microphones, amps, two mountains of speakers. I join Shelley on the stairs. That went well. As long as I hang on to the railing, it's cool.

I get my spot, up in the balcony, in the middle, in the front, where the sound really comes together and I pass out, my head dangling at a seemingly awkward angle. I am asleep. A hopeless case. Shelley is a flower in a field of pollinated weeds. I am shook again and I hear a familiar voice. It's Ricky.

"Little dude, don't go on the nod, man," Ricky says. "Do some crank!"

There's a spoon under my nose and I snort. The Scooter, that is Phil Rizzuto, is in my head, screaming "Holy Cow!" Ricky does up my other 'stril. My brain is active.

"We have to see Garcia!" Ricky says, and he's gone.

My head snaps up. My eyes open wide. I had forgotten about the concert. I gotta see Garcia. The warm-up act is already down there, a one-man band bizarrely encumbered by instruments. He's playing "All Along the Watchtower," and gets called back for an encore. That's pretty cool for a warm-up act, warming up for a be-loved artist. My head is perfect.

Nick and I look at each other and he says, "We are primed!"

"My guardian angel was Oakland chapter," I say with a laugh.

And Jerry came on stage with the JGB (Keith and Donna, John Kahn on bass, and Ron Tutt on drums). The special guest star *was* Maria Muldaur, who stood beside Donna and sang backup throughout the show. After a few moments of noodling over the catcalls of the crowd, Jerry began—bum, bum, bum BUM—the forty-five-minute "Sugaree."

"When they come to take you down . . ."

• • •

Thirty-seven years later, it seems like a dream, partying with Hells Angels, forty-five-minute "Sugarees," social experiments, and cliched attempts to discover America. So I looked for verification. There are websites that list every song played at every concert by the Dead, the JGB, RatDog, etc., etc. The Internet, if nothing else, is comprehensive. So it is a disappointment that the list for the August 6 JGB show at the Keystone Berkeley is partial—in fact, only four songs are listed, all supposedly from the second set. They are "Sugaree"; "Mystery Train," a cover of the Little Junior's Blue Flames song; "Simple Twist of Fate," the Dylan tune; and "Don't Let Go," a Roy Hamilton cover. My first instinct was that there had been some confusion, because "Sugaree" *was* the first set. But there were other problems as well. I remember "Knockin' on Heaven's Door," and I was positive that Maria Muldaur had been brought up to the front to sing her hit "Midnight at the Oasis." Oh well, I was in no condition to make a list that night and, apparently, neither was anyone else who was there. I did learn that Muldaur became a full-fledged member of the JGB for most of 1978. As for the Dead, no West Coast shows were planned, but there was a big concert in the works for the fall back East. I'd have to wait a few more weeks.

OF ENGLISHTOWN, AND THE
MYRIAD GLORIES OF '77

Nick stayed behind in San Francisco, and I returned east by Grey-hound Bus for my senior year at Hofstra. I sat in the back seat of the bus with Liz Shefrin, who was on her way east to visit a sick brother. She had Valium and I had Darvocet, so we stayed tranquil and pain-free in our spaceship. At night, heading through Kansas without a single light anywhere near, we might as well have been in space. Got back to Long Island just in time to drop my stuff off in my dorm room, have a Dead ticket miraculously appear in my hand, and catch a ride to Raceway Park in Englishtown, New Jersey, with a driver named Reefer John who drove like Jimmy Clark and once filled his radiator out of a puddle when it overheated just past the George Washington Bridge. In Englishtown the Dead played on my twenty-first birthday. It was hot, and while hoofing it in I was startled by the commerce going on. In Berkeley there was Jerry G Acid. In New Jersey there was an extended menu of substances you could use to get your head right. Had I been into hallucinogens (I was a beer and bong guy), I would have had my choice of ten different kinds of acid, mescaline, or psilocybin, which last were referred to by the vendors as "shrooms." The key for me was I didn't drink, which meant I wouldn't need a visit from my guardian angel to get through the show. The crowd was very rowdy, a little bit foul, but cheerful. After eight weeks in the Bay Area the New Jersey sun seemed hot and the kids loudmouthed.

There was still a lot of talk about the spring shows the Dead played at the Palladium, and the night the Hells Angels rode their Harleys right into the building and into the Dead's dressing room where they demanded to hear "Truckin'." They played great on 14th Street that week. The shows didn't meander and sputter as Dead shows had in the past. This was a band with an attention span and focus and, surprise, more focus! They played some songs for the first time. They debuted "Fire on the Mountain" as we know it today. They'd played it in the spring but it had different lyrics. "Estimated Prophet," a 7/4 reggae tune, made its debut, initially an assemblage of shards that popped up in jams or rehearsals, and formed a whole song that remained a staple for the rest of the band's days. There were a lot of holograph moments, every night they became a band with a mind of its own. All the vocalists were at the top of their game. Consensus was the band was tripping less and doing more primo blow. (In retrospect this remains a viable theory.) But the band was also tighter because it was better rehearsed, taken through their paces by record producer Keith Olsen, who had just finished up with Fleetwood Mac (at Wally Heider's), and was producing *Terrapin Station*.* As soon as the record was finished they went on tour, and their gig at Cornell's Barton Hall on May 8 was exceptional.† Days later, they played an intense "Sugaree" in St. Paul, Minnesota, and a superior "Wharf

---

*During one session John Belushi showed up, drank everything in sight, and passed out in front of the console.

†The Cornell show is still considered one of their best ever, the first night they ever played "Scarlet Begonias" and "Fire on the Mountain" back to back, creating the classic "Scar/Fire." There have been lots of polls taken of Deadheads asking what they think was the greatest Dead show ever, and the results are fairly consistent, says the *New York Times*, with the Cornell University show of May 8, 1977, and the February 13 and 14, 1970, shows at the Fillmore East. Tapes of these shows were also among the most heavily traded among expert collectors.

Rat" in Connecticut. Keith was playing very well, and jazz piano was giving the texture of old songs a new richness.

Not everyone understood the way I did that 1977 was a key year in the history of the Dead, Year One. There were those at the racetrack who remembered the peaks that came simultaneously with Pigpen's last hurrah, after they got back from Europe, on August 27, 1972, in Veneta, Oregon, the greatest "Dark Star" in history. And a lot of folks were East Coast and recalled May 2, 1970, in Binghamton, and the way they played "Dancing in the Street" all night.

There were guys at Englishtown who claimed to have inside information. In June, Mickey drove through a guardrail and busted himself up—but even the know-it-alls were ignorant of key facts that would only come out later. Phil was having trouble with his ol' lady and drinking beer for breakfast. Keith had found a strong form of heroin,* and receded like a hairline into a black hole that stole his art. Bill and Bobby also were dealing with breakups. On Mickey, at least, all that was broken was his arm, ribs, and collarbone.

The summer was just about over in Englishtown. Technically I was back at school. I wore cutoffs, Converse All Stars, and a red bandana. I had a sleeveless light denim shirt with me but it was hanging out of my back pocket.

This was the biggest deal ever for the Dead as the headline act. More than 100,000 tickets had been sold and everyone was

---

*Heroin had been a band thing since at least 1974 when they were introduced to "China White" in Europe. This new stuff was called "Persian," and you smoked it out of a pipe. At first everyone thought it was opium, but it turned out to be heroin, and it sent those who habitually smoked it into a dark place. Jerry especially took to smoking Persian in 1977, which he found went well with the edginess of coke. Years later, he got to a point where he was spending $700 a day on Persian, and setting his hotel rooms on fire.

there to see *them*. Many more than that showed up. The promoters were determined to keep freeloaders from overwhelming the event. There would be no gate-crashers. I was glad I was holding a ticket, as there were parts of the perimeter that were barricaded to resemble Omaha Beach on D-day. The stage was in a field, and I was directly in front of the stage, about a quarter of a mile back, which was better than some.

The warm-up bands were the Marshall Tucker Band and New Riders. I don't remember Marshall Tucker, sorry. I must have been otherwise occupied. The New Riders' set included "Panama Red," "Glendale Train," and "Dead Flowers." Won't forget to put roses on your gray-vuh.

I don't remember specifics of the Dead show, but I'll never forget how it felt. It was something that all of the records in the world couldn't have prepared me for, that first feeling of being safely cradled in the enveloping drift of one-band consciousness, alternately delicate and powerful, synchronized and fractious. It was also the largest crowd I'd ever been in, and I recall some anxiety when trying to relocate my friends (some of whom I'd only met that day) after a trip to the Johnny-on-the-Spot.

Luckily this time there was someone there with the wherewithal to write down the set. For my twenty-first birthday the Dead played, first set, "Promised Land," "They Love Each Other," "Me and My Uncle" "Mississippi Half-Step Uptown Toodeloo," "Looks Like Rain," "Peggy-O," "Minglewood Blues," "Friend of the Devil," "The Music Never Stopped"; second set, "Bertha," "Good Lovin'," "Loser," "Estimated Prophet," "Eyes of the World," "Samson and Delilah," "He's Gone," "Not Fade Away," "Truckin'"; encore, "Terrapin Station," the song Hunter said came to him on a beam, but kind of a sleepy finish to a long, hot day. I was with Jersey folks and the only one heading immediately back to school, so I got a ride as far as Newark in the back of a van, then took various commuter rails to Hempstead, where I arrived just in time to have my mug taken for that year's student ID.

And that was how it started for me. I had found Jerry and the forty-five-minute "Sugaree," and I'd found the Epicurean ataraxia of the Dead during what *Rolling Stone* would later call "The Grateful Dead's Greatest Year." I was content being just happy. Then it got better. Back at school I met Lisa, my future wife and mother of my children, and for my next few Dead shows I had a date.

33

WHEN JERRY DIED
THE VIBE LIVED ON

I found out at Yankee Stadium. August 9, 1995. The Yankees were playing the Baltimore Orioles in a matinee, and I was waiting in the will-call line to pick up my comps when photographer George Napolitano asked me if I'd heard. Heart attack. Died in his sleep in rehab, George said. It was a body blow, a shot to the gut, but I held it together. Everyone knew Jerry was in trouble.

Those who'd seen shows in the Grateful Dead's final tour were solemn when they spoke of the experience. Jerry was worse, much worse. We'd grown used to the hoarse voice, to his lack of wind, to the fact that he looked seventy-five but was really fifty-two, but at Soldier Field in Chicago at the last show in July, Jerry had been really shaky.

You can watch the whole show on YouTube if you want, and truth is, Jerry's voice had sounded worse than it did that night. But it had never sounded sadder. When he sang his last two tunes, "So Many Roads" and "Black Muddy River," it sounded so much like goodbye that it scared people. He sounded in mourning as he sang, "So many roads I tell you / from New York to San Francisco / all I want is one / to take me home." At song's end his voice cracks with what sounds like a sob. And then, in the first song of a two-song encore, "When it seems like the night will last forever / and there's nothing left to do but count the years / when the strings of my heart start to sever* / and stones fall from my eyes instead of tears / I will walk alone by the black muddy river / and dream me a dream of my own."

He sang those songs like he knew it was the last time, and maybe he did. Jerry had long associated the music he made with his immortality, that when his physical form went away, his song, the song he put up into the air for everyone to hear, would linger on. Hunter naturally never wanted to define what he meant by the black muddy river. Hint: It wasn't a real river. The lyricist said the best way to get it was to ponder on the "archetypal subconscious resonances" of the image. Jerry no doubt felt it was important which were his last songs, and he chose songs that he could best slide inside and extend his stay. In his book *Garcia: A Signpost to New Space*, Jerry said, "Music has infinite space. You can go as far into the music as you can fill a million lifetimes." The Grateful Dead had been built to last, not just to create music in the moment but to create a legacy for the musicians. And Jerry was, according to Rock Scully, an evocative assemblage of contradictions. He was a "gullible hipster, ironic Utopian, self-effacing star," and a recluse who lived for the current of energy between himself and an audience.

But those are retrospective thoughts. According to David Vecsey, who was there, the show "creaked and crawled and just finally petered out, with Garcia barely contributing in a truncated second set." Everything . . . was . . . slow. It was the end of a long stretch of problems with Jerry. In the spring they'd tried to cut a studio record and couldn't because Jerry was a chronic no-show.

*Robert Hunter is superimposing Jerry's actual heart, the one that would give out in a month, with his guitar, his preferred method of expressing love, raised consciousness, and art. When it came time for the guitar solo in that final version of "Black Muddy River," Jerry stuck startlingly to the simple melody.

For concerts, he showed up, but he was slothful on stage, avoiding eye contact, and missing cues. The last song, the last song of the last show, was "Box of Rain," the existential masterpiece, Phil Lesh singing Robert Hunter's words, "For this is all a dream we dreamed / one afternoon long ago / . . . Such a long, long time to be gone / and a short time to be there," and doing it because he couldn't stand the idea of closing the tour with one of Jerry's saddest songs.

Truth was, it had been a long time since the band sparked. If you saw a great Dead show in the 1990s you were very lucky. The whole telepathy thing had worn off or been forgotten or something. They would try to jam and nothing would happen. It was like the worst of the acid-test days when they'd melt down and everybody loved it, only now they were in a packed stadium in front of 60,000 people and nobody could even figure out what key they were in. There were times when the jams would sputter and stop, and the lights would go out, just so the audience wouldn't be able to see the train wreck.

I was on the East Coast where reactions to Jerry's passing were muted, where we let FM disc jockeys do the talking for us, and wondered what was going to fill that gaping void we felt with Jerry gone. It was certainly the end of the Dead, right? How could they play without Jerry, whose rhapsodic solos wafted across the hypnotic nights of our lives like a lovely yet complex smoke, whose voice whether sweet with youth or weatherworn from the road, sounded perfect to us even when it clearly was not?

It was out West where the real stuff was going on, just as it had always been. With no public announcement, no attempts to *organize*, folks were drawn spontaneously to the Polo Fields in Golden Gate Park in San Francisco, putting fresh flowers in their graying hair, and the long-held notion that the Dead were a religion, and Jerry its priest, began to manifest itself in handmade altars.

Some of the grander gestures were compliments of Bill Graham Presents, which sent a thirty-foot portrait of Jerry playing guitar. Members of the band showed up, and paraded around beating impromptu percussion instruments. Some brought their guitars and drums and an endless jam session ensued, "Friend of the Devil" being played in an endless loop like Shari Lewis's "The Song That Never Ends" (written by Norman Martin).

Mickey addressed the gathering, "It's up to you now," he said. "Take what he gave you and *do something* with it."

On Market Street, where I'd traipsed up and down the brick sidewalks during my first pilgrimage to see Jerry, there was a tall flagpole flanked by shorter poles outside city hall, overlooking the Civic Center Plaza, a main pole where the American flag typically flew. Instead of lowering the flag to half mast, as they might've done had any other notable local passed, the red, white, and blue was taken down completely, and replaced with a tie-dyed flag, waving wide and high. The flags on the shorter poles were lowered to half-staff. One glimpse of that and no one had to ask who died. And it was even more noteworthy because it was tribute offered by the local *government* to Planet Jerry, a place where it often had no jurisdiction, a tribute by a government that had once feared Garcia and the army of hippies who followed him, but that now recognized the Dead as one of the city's greatest goodwill ambassadors.

As the news sunk in, there was a feeling that it was more than the music that was gone, but the hippie epoch itself, with its intrinsic judgment-free zones, bad-trip tents, and antiauthoritarianism. A careful look at history shows that the Summer of '67 in San Francisco was an actual turning point in American history, a time when upward of 100,000 young people descended on a city, not because of a dust bowl, a Great Depression, or a natural disaster, but because of a soul-sucking social ennui. It was an outgrowth of World War II and the Cold War, eras when military aggression and strength were considered the answer to all foreign-policy questions. A new generation born after the bombs fell on Nagasaki and Hiroshima, and fed up with the nightmares of mushroom clouds out their classroom windows, rebelled against the ways of their elders. Long hair and untidiness wasn't just laziness but a conscious antimilitary statement. The conservatism of the 1950s gave way like a bursting dam to a new sexual freedom (the invention of the birth-control pill helped, too). The pleasant side effects of drugs developed by the government during "mind-control experiments," and smokables previously used predominantly by jazz musicians and beatniks, proved to be catnip to the newfangled heads filled with liberal thought. The movement was portrayed on TV as sensual and idealistic—if it feels good do it, make love not war—and sure enough it started out that way, but in reality the search for Shangri-La went awry rather abruptly, meandering off course into hellish addiction, violence, and shattered dreams of all sorts. Sure, Altamont and Manson plunged the dagger into the hippie's heart, but the scene was already moribund, damaged by the same flaws in the human spirit that stain all ideals: sadism, greed, lust. But that was reality. In the imaginations of young Americans, of which I was one in 1977 heading west to find *whatever*, it was the dream that lived on, lives on, and the Grateful Dead were that dream's traveling troubadours.

After a while, the people on Market Street, and those in the park, stopped their dervish dance long enough to look at each other, and realized that this thing that had happened was a party! How appropriate.

Country Joe McDonald, sans Fish, felt all alone. He felt angry. Those in a position to help stood by and let Jerry kill himself. When intervention was called for, Jerry's friends sat mute. Jerry could have been *saved*, he said.

Maybe. Probably not. Jerry was a guy who hadn't done a sit-up since the army. He lived on hot dogs and milk shakes, smoked three packs a day. And of course, mind alteration was for him a science as well as an art. The chances that he was going to reinvent himself as a jogger, or a guy who stuck to salads and sobriety, seem remote at best.

Jerry said it best, "I'm really not that much into my physical self."

His body was a necessity and he knew he had to keep it alive in order to keep his mind alive. But it was a drag, tending toward the fat and blobby, a pain every time he had to schlep it around, which was all the time because he was a goddamn traveling musician.

He crammed a lot into his fifty-three years. So many roads. He was all used up.

The nurse went to check on him because he'd stopped snoring, which had never happened before, and found him with a smile on his face.

. . .

Back at Yankee Stadium, where Baltimore was thrashing New York 7–2, it was a sad day, much sadder than the days that would follow, because Jerry was gone and I didn't know, from my spot behind the Yankee dugout, if the vibe would live on. I hoped, but I didn't know what the people in Golden Gate Park already knew —it would survive.

Jerry's funeral service was held at St. Stephen's Church in Belvedere. Bob Dylan came. Jerry's ashes were sprinkled into the Pacific off the side of a boat. Too bad there was domestic bullshit marring the event, Mountain Girl not allowed to board the boat because the wife and the ex-wife didn't get along. When some of Jerry's ashes were caught by the wind and blown back against the side of the boat, Bobby Weir got soaked leaning over the edge to wipe them up with a napkin, and the napkin ended up buried in a field behind Phil's house.

children of skeletons

a sea of people surround me and how i love these children of skeletons still fresh with flesh dancing on the bones of the dead, these ancient graves beneath our feet that feed the seeds that breed the roses blooming in our heads, that breathe life into us so that we may swoon and sway to the music of today, dance this dance of life before we too wither and decay, yes, today we are grateful just to be alive and we extend that gratitude to the legions of the dead for it is on their broken backs that we dance and it is for them we have these roses and our share of the daily bread.

Jen Fountain (Chinacat Sunflower), 2014

THE MUSIC NEVER STOPS

As I sit here writing my Grateful Dead book, discussing cosmic events a half century old, I wasn't expecting *breaking news*. Minutes ago (today is January 16, 2015, 10:00 a.m.), I received an e-mail from the Dead announcing that Mickey, Bill, Phil, Bobby, Bruce Hornsby, with guests Trey Anastasio (uh oh, of Phish) and Jeff Chimenti (of RatDog, Further, the Other Ones), will be playing three shows at Chicago's Soldier Field on July 3, 4, and 5, 2015. The event is called "Fare Thee Well: Celebrating 50 Years of the Grateful Dead."

The announcement came with a couple of quotes.

Mickey said, "I have a feeling this will come out just right. Can't wait to find out. . . . Here we go!"

Bill said, "The Grateful Dead lived an incredible musical story and now we get to write a whole new chapter. By celebrating our 50th, we get to cheer our past, but this isn't just about history. The Grateful Dead always played improvisational music that was born in the moment and we plan on doing the same this round."

Well, the announcement was only minutes old when social media began to explode with outrage. How dare they? Trey? The Treyful Dead? It was capitalism at its worst. Just wait. Ticket prices were going to explode. Only millionaires would be able to go.

The Deadheads on my social network don't like Phish and they don't like Trey. They don't like Warren Haynes either, but not as bad as they hate Trey.

The Soldier Field tickets sold, many to scalpers,* and everyone was getting in on the act. Fiftieth anniversary, of what? Maybe when they changed their name from the Warlocks or something. Nobody knew. It was the fiftieth anniversary!

A custom-guitar maker known as Alvarez used the GD fan site on the Internet to introduce Grateful Dead guitars for sale, limited-edition signature guitars, replete with official artwork applied with innovative printing techniques, mother-of-pearl inlay, rosewood fingerboard, bi-level bridge, A-grade western red cedar top, and twelfth-fret lightning bolt.

In February Bobby gave an interview to CNBC's Steve Liesman. Told that there was quite a fuss caused by the announcement of the concert, Bobby said, "I've heard that's been pretty monstrous, gratifying, but at the same time, we'd better be good!"

Asked about the controversy with regard to Trey, Bobby said, "After kicking around who's going to work best, it should be pretty evident to anyone who doesn't have a serious ax to grind who we should be dancing with here." Bobby firmly pro-Trey.

There was another fuss in March when the *Chicago Tribune* reported that Deadheads would not be allowed to camp outside Soldier Field before and after the show, a move construed by Deadheads as (*a*) unwise, and (*b*) a surefire sign that the PTB were trying to keep out the riffraff.

The news kept coming. In February 2015 it was announced that during the spring Jerry Garcia and Robert Hunter would be inducted into the Songwriters' Hall of Fame at the Marriott Marquis Hotel in New York.

*By the end of February 2015, a UPI reporter with the disturbing name of Thor Benson wrote that tickets for Fare Thee Well were selling for $15,000. The Deadheads were right. Many millionaires in the crowd, a middleman getting the money. Now Bobby's talking about ways so everyone can enjoy the show, so I'm expecting a pay-per-view announcement.

In March it was announced that a concert entitled "Dear Jerry," celebrating the music of Jerry Garcia, would be held on May 14, at a campground in Maryland halfway between Baltimore and Washington, well before the Chicago show, featuring all surviving band members plus Jorma.

These are all surefire signs that the Grateful Dead still matter, along with this: somewhere at this exact moment in the multiverse—the many simultaneous somewheres prophesied by physics, chemically induced by Owsley, imagined by Hunter, given voice by the Dead, and lived by you and me—somewhere somebody is listening to the Grateful Dead. A high school kid in New Jersey is spinning in her room. An old hippie in Mendocino drops the needle in a well-worn groove. A garage band in Oklahoma takes their time tuning because they love. And a trucker, crossing the alkali flats of a great desert late at night, spins the dial and pulls in a signal: sweet as blossoms blooming, clear as a ripple on still water; channeling our bliss, connecting the dots, finding the music that plays the band.

The music never stops.

Acknowledgments

I would like to thank the following individuals
without whose help the writing of this book would have
been impossible: Larry Beck, Ed Behringer, Tekla Benson,
Jay Bianchi, Keith Brenner, Chris Carr, Anne Darrigan, my great
agent Jake Elwell of Harold Ober Associates, Rick Erickson,
Jen "Chinacat Sunflower" Fountain, Scott Frommer, Lisa Grasso,
Mark Harris, editor extraordinaire Stephen P. Hull, Jake Martin
of Dupree's Diamond Dealer, Grateful Dead archivist
Nicholas Meriwether, Nick Newlin, Gregg and Pam Praetorius,
John Scher, Jay Schukoske, Carl Soloway, Spliffany,
Nathan Versace, and Charlene Wrobel.

Further Reading

BOOKS

Allen, Scott W. *Aces Back to Back: The History of the Grateful Dead, 1965–2013*. Parker, CO: Outskirts Press, 2014.

Brightman, Carol. *Sweet Chaos: The Grateful Dead's American Adventure*. New York: Clarkson Potter Publishers, 1998.

Dodd, David G. *The Complete Annotated Grateful Dead Lyrics*. New York: Free Press, 2007.

Gans, David. *Conversations with the Dead: The Grateful Dead Interview Book*. Boston: Da Capo Press, 2002.

Garcia, Jerry, Charles Reich, and Jann Wenner. *Garcia: A Signpost to New Space*. Boston: Da Capo Press, 2003.

Gimbel, Steve. *The Grateful Dead and Philosophy: Getting High Minded about Love and Haight*. Chicago: Open Court Publishing Company, 2007.

Greenfield, Robert. *Dark Star: An Oral Biography of Jerry Garcia*. New York: It Books, 2009.

Harrison, Hank. *The Dead*. Millbrae, CA: Celestial Arts, 1980.

Hofmann, Albert. *LSD: My Problem Child*. New York: McGraw-Hill, 1980.

Lang, Michael, with Holly George-Warren. *The Road to Woodstock*. New York: Ecco, 2003.

Lesh, Phil. *Searching for the Sound: My Life with the Grateful Dead*. New York: Back Bay Books, 2006.

McNally, Dennis. *A Long Strange Trip: The Inside Story of the Grateful Dead*. New York: Three Rivers Press, 2014.

Meriwether, Nicholas, ed. *All Graceful Instruments: The Contexts of the Grateful Dead Phenomenon*. Newcastle-upon-Tyne, UK: Cambridge Scholars Publishing, 2007.

———. *Reading the Grateful Dead: A Critical Study*. Lanham, MD: Scarecrow Press, 2012.

———. *Studying the Dead: The Grateful Dead Scholars Caucus, An Informal History*. Lanham, MD: Scarecrow Press, 2013.

Rifken, Glenn, and Sam Hill. *Radical Marketing: From Harvard to Harley, Lessons from Ten That Broke the Rules and Made It Big*. New York: HarperBusiness, 2000.

Ruhlmann, William. *The History of the Grateful Dead*. New York: Gallery Books, 1990.

Scully, Rock, and David Dalton. *Living with the Dead: Twenty Years on the Bus with Garcia and the Grateful Dead*. Lanham, MD: Cooper Square Press, 2001.

Wenner, Jann S., ed. *Grateful Dead: The Ultimate Guide*. New York: Rolling Stone, 2004.

NEWSPAPERS AND MAGAZINES

Blinstein, Jon. "Phil Lesh and Bob Weir Disband Further." *Rolling Stone*, November 4, 2014. Accessed February 7, 2015; http://www.rollingstone .com/music/news/furthur-call-quits-ahead-grateful-deads-50th -anniversary-20141104.

Brennan, James. "Orchestra's Rapport with Rock Band Electrifies Audience." *Buffalo Evening News*, March 18, 1970.

Briscoe, Tony. "No Camping Outside Soldier Field for Grateful Dead Fans." *Chicago Tribune*, March 3, 2015.

Browne, David. "In the Dark." *Rolling Stone*, August 13, 1987. Accessed December 29, 2014; http://www.rollingstone.com/music /albumreviews/in-the-dark-19870813.

———. "Grateful Dead Lyricist Robert Hunter Set for Rare Tour." *Rolling Stone*, September 25, 2013. Accessed January 25, 2015; http://www .rollingstone.com/music/news/grateful-dead-lyricist-robert-hunter -set-for-rare-tour-20130925.

———. "The Grateful Dead's Greatest Year." *Rolling Stone*, June 26, 2013. Accessed January 21, 2015; http://www.rollingstone.com/music/news /the-grateful-deads-greatest-year-20130626.

DeMatteis, J. M. "Go to Heaven." *Rolling Stone*, August 7, 1980. Accessed December 29, 2014; http://www.rollingstone.com/music /albumreviews/go-to-heaven-19800807.

Dodd, David. "The Annotated 'Ripple.'" Accessed January 13, 2015; http://artsites.ucsc.edu/GDead/agdl/ripple.html.

Dougherty, Steve. "What a Long, Strange Trip." *People*, August 21, 1995. Accessed February 4, 2015; http://www.people.com/people/archive /article/0,20101375,00.html.

Dowling, William C. "'Ripple': A Minor Excursus." The Annotated Grateful Dead Lyrics website. Accessed January 13, 2015; artsites .ucsc.edu.

Eisen, Benjy. "Bob Weir on the Dead's 50th Anniversary: 'We Owe It to the Songs.'" *Rolling Stone*, January 30, 2014. Accessed December 29, 2014; http://www.rollingstone.com/music/news/bob-weir-on-the -deads-50th-anniversary-we-owe-it-to-the-songs-20140130.

Gilmore, Mikal. "Jerry Garcia: 1942–1995." *Rolling Stone*, September 21, 1995. Accessed December 30, 2014; http://www.rollingstone.com /music/news/jerry-garcia-1942-1995-19950921.

Greenfield, Robert. "Owsley Stanley: The King of LSD." *Rolling Stone*, March 14, 2011. Accessed February 20, 2015; http://www.rollingstone .com/culture/news/owsley-stanley-the-king-of-lsd-20110314.

Grow, Kory. "Bob Weir Cancels All Upcoming RatDog Performances through 2015." *Rolling Stone*, August 11, 2014. Accessed December 29, 2014; http://www.rollingstone.com/music/news/bob-weir-cancels-all -upcoming-ratdog-performances-through-2015-20140811.

Martin, Douglas. "Rock Scully, Grateful Dead's Manager Who Put the Band on Records, Dies at 73." *New York Times*, December 21, 2014, A36.

Ratliff, Ben. "Bring Out Your Dead." *New York Times*, April 10, 2009. Accessed January 25, 2015; http://www.nytimes.com/2009/04/12/arts /music/12ratl.html?pagewanted=all&_r=0.

Vecsey, David. "The Day Jerry Garcia Died." *New York Times*, August 9, 2013. Accessed December 30, 2014; http://6thfloor.blogs.nytimes .com/2013/08/09/the-day-jerry-garcia-died/.

Veltman, Chloe. "Paying Tribute to the Grateful Dead in Symphony." *Los Angeles Times*, August 5, 2009.

Von Tersch, Gary. "Shakedown Street." *Rolling Stone*, March 8, 1979. Accessed December 29, 2014; http://www.rollingstone.com/music /albumreviews/shakedown-street-19790308.

Beauchamp, Scott, "Sometimes We Live No Particular Way But Our Own: The Grateful Dead and Epicureanism." Accessed January 20, 2015; http://www.full-stop.net/2013/04/20/features/scott-beauchamp/sometimes-we-live-no-particular-way-but-our-own-the-grateful-dead-and-epicureanism/.

Benson, Thor. "Tickets for Grateful Dead Reunion Being Sold for Nearly $15,000." Accessed March 1, 2015; http://www.upi.com/Odd_news/2015/02/28/Tickets-for-Grateful-Dead-reunion-being-sold-for-nearly-15000/6001425157505/.

"Jerry's Guitars." Accessed January 13, 2015; http://dozin.com/jers/guitar/history.htm.

Hardman, Chris. "10 of the Best: The Grateful Dead." Accessed January 26, 2015; http://www.theguardian.com/music/musicblog/2014/apr/02/10-of-the-best-the-grateful-dead.

Meriwether, Nicholas G. "Revisiting Cornell '77." Rock and Roll Hall of Fame Museum. Accessed January 25, 2015; rockhall.com.

"UCSC's Grateful Dead Archivist." Interview with Nicholas Meriwether. Accessed January 28, 2015; http://www.ilovelibraries.org/article/ucscs-grateful-dead-archivist.

MICHAEL BENSON has published more than sixty books, wears a "Steal Your Face" hoodie, attended dozens of Dead shows, and still roots for the Lithuanian basketball team during the Summer Olympics. His books include *Vintage Science Fiction Films*, *Who's Who in the JFK Assassination*, *Ballparks of North America*, *Inside Secret Societies*, and *Killer Twins*. Benson graduated with honors from Hofstra University on Long Island, where he was for four years a rock critic for the *Hofstra Chronicle*. His collaborators include a biker, a spy, a pro wrestler, an astronaut, and an NFL Hall of Famer. He is currently a regular on-screen contributor to the *Evil Twins* and *Evil Kin* television programs shown on the Investigation Discovery (I.D.) Channel, and lives in Brooklyn, New York.